# The Student Survival Guide for Research Methods in Psychology

*The Student Survival Guide for Research Methods in Psychology* is designed to support students enrolled in undergraduate or graduate level research methods courses by providing them with the tools they need to succeed. It goes beyond course material to help students engage more fully with research methods content.

This survival guide presents clear step-by-step instructions that will help students hone the basic skills to succeed and thrive in their research methods classes and to navigate common pitfalls. The book covers core practical skills, like formatting and writing at an APA standard, understanding research literature (particularly academic journals), using SPSS, and broader skills like how to communicate with your professor, time management, and teamwork skills.

It is a highly effective primer text for all psychology students undertaking research methods courses and will also be particularly helpful for students who are currently undertaking these modules and don't feel fully prepared for them.

**Ross A. Seligman** has been teaching research methods and other psychology classes for over 28 years. Apart from Citrus College, he has also taught at Pasadena City College, Mt. San Antonio College, and Chaffey College in California. Ross is also an experienced department chair and dean. He has a Bachelor of Arts in psychology from Occidental

College and a Master of Arts in clinical psychology from California State University, Los Angeles. Ross also did his doctoral coursework in social psychology at the Claremont Graduate University in Claremont, CA.

**Lindsay A. Mitchell** recently graduated from California State University, Fullerton, USA, with her bachelor's degree in Psychology.

# The Student Survival Guide for Research Methods in Psychology

Ross A. Seligman and Lindsay A. Mitchell

Routledge
Taylor & Francis Group

NEW YORK AND LONDON

First published 2022
by Routledge
605 Third Avenue, New York, NY 10158

and by Routledge
2 Park Square, Milton Park, Abingdon, Oxon, OX14 4RN

*Routledge is an imprint of the Taylor & Francis Group, an informa business*

© 2022 Taylor & Francis

*Library of Congress Cataloging-in-Publication Data*
A catalog record for this book has been requested

ISBN: 978-0-367-56803-0 (hbk)
ISBN: 978-0-367-56251-9 (pbk)
ISBN: 978-1-003-09936-9 (ebk)

DOI: 10.4324/9781003099369

Typeset in Bembo
by Apex CoVantage, LLC

This book was written during the safer at home orders in the US during the Covid-19 pandemic. Both Ross and Lindsay would like to dedicate this book to the over 2.5 million people that have lost their lives to Covid-19 worldwide. Ross would also like to dedicate this book to his father, who passed from natural causes during the writing of this book.

# Contents

# 1 Overview

## How This Book Will Help You Survive Research Methods

Greetings and welcome to class! You have probably purchased this book because you are taking a research methods class for psychology students and want to do well in it. The purpose of this book is to guide you through your research methods course and help you get the outcome that you desire. This book is designed to take you through every step of the class, helping you understand the topics that your professor will be presenting to you, by providing both a professor and a student's point of view on the subject matter. Before discussing the topics covered in this book, let me start off with some introductions.

My name is Ross A. Seligman, and I have been teaching college- and university-level research methods classes for psychology students for over 25 years. I would like to use the experience that I have gained from teaching this class to help you succeed.

DOI: 10.4324/9781003099369-1

Next, I would like to introduce you to my co-author, Lindsay A. Mitchell. Lindsay was a student of mine a few years back at Citrus College in Glendora, California. When Lindsay took my research methods class, she not only had a deep understanding as well as a passion for research but was also very supportive of the other students in the class and a good group leader. For those reasons, I asked her to write this book with me.

Lindsay now has a bachelor's degree in psychology from California State University in Fullerton. She is applying to research-based graduate programs in the hopes of continuing on to get her master's degree in cognitive neuroscience. Lindsay will be writing her parts of this book from an empathetic student perspective. Think of her as a supportive guide and friend who is there to help you get through each part of this course. Most chapters in this book will be written by both of us so that you will be able to gain insight and knowledge from both sides of the classroom. That way, you can better understand what your professor expects from you while also benefiting from the thoughts of a fellow student who can help you understand and meet the challenges of the class.

With introductions completed, let me tell you a bit more about this book and how it will help you. Ideally, you should read the first three chapters of this book before you even start your research methods course. It has been designed to help make your research methods class more predictable and seem more manageable. We will start off with the basic topic of communicating with your professor. Some of you may already be excellent at this task; however, there are situations that you might encounter in which you might not know the best way to respond. This book will help you handle those difficult situations.

Lindsay and I will teach you excellent communication skills as well as the correct method and time to use them. For example, what should you do if you are not happy with your grade on an assignment? How do you respond? What if you have missed several assignments but feel you have good reasons for missing them? What should you do? These questions and much more will be discussed in Chapter 2.

The goal of Chapter 3 is to prepare you to succeed in the class before it has even really begun. This chapter will introduce you to some of the different types of assignments that you will find in this class (such as labs, tests, experimental write-ups, group projects, etc.) as well as other obstacles that you might face (working with groups, applying difficult concepts to real world situations, hands-on projects, etc.). When you take your first research methods course, there is a very good chance that you will have to carry out a full-scale research project either on your own or with a group of your peers. This can be a daunting project, but Lindsay and I will give you the information that you need to succeed on not only this project but also similar ones that you may encounter later on in your educational career.

As I previously mentioned, your research methods class may require group work. For example, in my class there are weekly group activities that I have my students engage in, along with a group project, that last the entire term. This project involves working with four to five other people over the course of the term to design and carry out a full-scale experiment. Once the experiment is complete, the next task is to complete an APA-style experimental write-up. Not only is the project itself a bit stressful and very time consuming, it is often met with interpersonal issues which arise due to group dynamics and can make the project even more complicated. In Chapter 4, we will teach you some strategies for working with a small and diverse group of individuals. We will focus on how to get the best possible outcomes from your group and how to handle problems when they occur.

One of the biggest tasks you will be immediately faced with is under-standing and applying some difficult terms. Your professor will most likely explain these terms to you during your lecture sessions, but if you find that you are in need of further assistance, then take a look at Chapter 5. There we will define and explain some of these difficult terms using words and examples that you hopefully find more familiar and understandable.

After discussing communication skills, working in small groups, and some of the difficult terms you will be required to learn, we will move on to focus on additional skills that you will use in almost every week of the course: finding, reading, and understanding good quality peer-reviewed psychology journal articles. It is likely that one of the first assignments you will be asked to complete in your research methods class is to find, read, and summarize a peer-reviewed psychology journal article. This is an important task to learn because you will be reading many journal articles throughout the rest of your class. We will help teach you how to identify a good quality peer-reviewed journal article as well as how to understand the language in each section before summarizing the article in your own words.

Chapter 7 will discuss in depth the nature of weekly experimental labs that you may have to work on in class. These labs are often a substantial part of your grade. This is where you will find that your research methods class is a little bit different than most other lower division psychology classes, as each class period will be composed of both a lecture component and a lab component. You are all probably most familiar with the lecture component of classes, during which you listen, discuss, and take notes on informa-tion that your professor provides for you. However, during the lab compo-nent you will be carrying out various types of activities like designing and conducting simple experiments and surveys, reading and analyzing journal articles, and other research-related projects. The labs often require you to understand difficult concepts and apply them to real-world settings. You may also be asked to write a several page paper each week during the lab period and complete it before you leave for the day. This is the most impor-tant part of the class, in my opinion, because it is the time in which you will absorb most of the information that is presented to you by your professor.

The later chapters will shift gears a little bit to focus more on the hard skills needed for the class, which will all be necessary for the completion of your term project. Depending on your college, graduate school, and/or professor, the details of the final project may vary. However, for most colleges and universities, the project has the same basic structure. You will be creating a hypothesis, designing and conducting an experiment or similar research project, analyzing your data, and writing up a full APA experimental paper that will include a literature review, methods, results, and discussion sections, followed by references and appendices. This project will usually account for about half of your grade in the class, so that is why we have designated so much time to helping you through completing each of the sections needed in your written paper.

At the end of the term, after you have finished your experiment and turned in your paper, you may then have to present your findings in front of your peers. Your presentation will involve you and/or your group standing in front of the class and discussing your project orally with the help of a poster or PowerPoint presentation slide deck. For many students, this type of presentation can be intimidating. Chapter 14 will teach you how to give an effective oral presentation that demonstrates your knowledge while also making it fun and engaging for your audience. This chapter will also address the most common mistakes that people make when giving oral presentations and how you can avoid them.

The final chapter is intended for students with interest in continuing their education and careers in the field of research psychology. At this point, Lindsay and I will share some opportunities available to you based on your interest in research psychology. Topics in the chapter include courses and degrees needed to pursue a career in the field, as well as some of the most popular careers that are currently available to you once you complete your education. There are many great types of careers out there waiting for you which will benefit from the ideas that your bright minds can bring to the field.

With this overview of the book in hand, it is time to begin our journey through the course! Lindsay and I strongly recommend that you read the next two chapters of this *Survival Guide* before you delve into your research methods course. We believe that this will start you off in the right direction and set you up for the most successful term possible.

# 2  Communicating With Your Professor

## Lindsay's Introduction

Hello there! My name is Lindsay, and as my colleague previously mentioned, I am a recent graduate from the psychology program at Cal State Fullerton. Although you know a little bit about me already, I would like to give you a bit more insight on the last few years of my college career.

I began at Citrus College in 2014 immediately following my graduation from high school. I started out interested in child development and the possibility of teaching K–12 public schooling. After two years, however, I began to feel uncertain and shifted my focus to psychology, a discipline that I was briefly exposed to in high school. After taking my first introductory psychology course, my curiosity and passion for understanding the human mind set me on a path that has gotten me to where I am today, with

DOI: 10.4324/9781003099369-2

a bachelor's degree and plans to continue on to complete graduate studies focused on research in cognitive neuroscience.

I met Ross during my last semester at Citrus College, as he was the professor for my introductory research methods course. I remember sitting down my first day of class feeling a bit nervous, as I was well aware of the difficulty of the class I was to begin. But in all honestly, I remember feeling mostly intrigued and excited, as I was finally going to be able to start a class that I was really interested in. I know what you're probably already thinking … "This girl is a bit looney. How can she be excited for research methods?!" Even Ross might have thought so after I walked up to him following our first class session and started going off about how passionate I was to learn how to do research and become a researcher myself one day. He later told me, after we became colleagues, that he had taken me for a bit of a brownnoser at the time, as most students tended to dread his class rather than look forward to it due to its more intense and difficult nature. Of course, once we got to know each other a bit better, he came to understand, as I do, that my elation toward research methods was rooted in my fascination for how psychologists have provided us with the immense amount of knowledge we currently have about human behavior. It was already clear to me that psychologists have come to their conclusions through research, but what I wondered was how they actually DO research. In other words, how do psychologists go from a simple research question to designing a study that can give them viable information? And the answer to this driving question of mine shortly began to be answered as I ventured through the class, as I hope it will also be answered for you.

Now that you know a bit more about me, let's get talking a bit more about the primary focus of this chapter: **communicating with your professor**. Now, as you may already have gathered from my first interaction with my introductory research methods professor, individuals often do not perfectly see eye to eye when conversing for the first time. As a student, it can be intimidating and worrisome to speak to your new professor for the first time for this very reason, among others. It can be even more nerve-wracking to raise your hand and speak up in class to ask or answer a question, which is a topic we will touch on here shortly. Throughout this chapter, we will go over various methods of communication that you can use to open up a conversation with your professor, including both in-person and remote interactions. I will also include some of my personal thoughts and tips regarding each one as we go along.

## Communicating With Your Professor

Before we get too deep into talking about one-on-one communication techniques, I would like to start by discussing an issue that may be a bit more personally relatable for you. Throughout your time in high school and/or college, how have you felt about speaking up in class or approaching your teachers and professors? If you have more of an outgoing and socially centered personality, then this has probably come quite naturally to you. But, as I personally believe, the social constructs put in place for us when we were young and learning how to be "proper" students have led most of us to tend to be more on the shy or quiet side when it comes to speaking up in the classroom. So, for those of you who feel hesitant or maybe even anxious and frightened to speak up either during class or afterwards when attempting to approach your professor, know that you are not alone in how you feel. Many students experience a similar feeling, including yours truly, who after six years of college still occasionally gets anxious about speaking up in class.

I have always been a bit on the quiet side, especially as a student, as I developed a strong fear within the classroom at a very young age that has stuck with me all these years. I do not know where it stemmed from, but for as long as I can remember, I have been absolutely terrified of sounding silly or, as I phrase it more harshly in my mind, "stupid" in front of my peers and teachers. I am sure it may be a bit of an egotistical thing to some extent, as many of my family members have been on the prideful side, regrettably to the level of self-destruction in some accounts. Regardless of its origin, this fear of mine has persisted throughout my life and only seemed to intensify over time. It led me to take on a state of complete silence in the classroom as I tried to the best of my ability to shrink as far into nothingness as I could, at the same desk I always chose in the corner of the room. The way I saw it, if I didn't say anything at all, then no one could use any of my words against me ... right? Well, although this tactic worked for me throughout high school, I found as I entered college that this perhaps was not the perfect solution that I once thought it was.

When I first started at Citrus College, I thought that I could do what I had always done and just keep quiet, with the sole intention of protecting myself by remaining as invisible as possible to my peers and professors. For my first couple of classes this worked for me, but I very soon began to notice a key difference between high school teachers and college professors. After asking a question to the class, I found that high school teachers would wait about 10 to 15 seconds (maybe even 20 seconds if they were feeling extra inquisitive that day) for a student to raise their hand before answering their question themselves and moving forward with the lecture with what seemed like a desperate need to stick to their schedule. In college, however, I found that professors did not treat their time with the same rushed and sometimes impatient attitude as my previous teachers. Instead, I started to notice that they would ask a question and just wait ... and wait ... and wait. Often, they would stare directly into the faces of their students with the sternest look on their faces, waiting for one brave soul to break the ever-growing awkward silence building in the room. And after just enough tension built, the professor would stubbornly say something like, "Come on guys, don't make me wait here all day." And shortly thereafter a student would offer up something ... anything to break the silence and get the professor to continue forward.

These elongated silences were what eventually persuaded me to begin speaking up more in class, as they soon perturbed me more than the thought of possibly making a fool of myself by asking a "dumb" question or answering one incorrectly. Before long, I came to realize another important idea that has since allowed me to get over my fear of social embarrassment and justify my choices of speaking up in class (even when I do ask perhaps a bit of a silly question or answer one poorly). And that idea was this: whether I take a backseat to my education or be an agent of what I want to learn, I was still paying what seemed to be solid gold bars to be there. I then had to make a decision ... Was I going to pay for silence? Was I going to let my peers decide for me what questions were worth discussing? Or was I going to step up and take charge of my own education? Because, in all honesty, I did not want to arrive at my graduation day and feel as though I had cruised quietly through my education, but never asked the questions I wanted to ask or provide some kind of answers for myself, my peers, and my professors. Since then, I have realized one more key truth that I would like to share with you here ... I came to understand that my questions were often ones that other students like me were also wondering about, and the questions that I responded to may have been useful in some way to the learning of not only myself but also my peers. I learned that my thoughts were worth sharing and that perhaps they could do good for more than just myself. Now, whenever I find the courage to share my thoughts in front of those around me, I know that even if I do make a fool of myself, I have the potential to provide a learning experience for not only myself but also my fellow students. And at least I can leave that day knowing I was brave enough to try rather than shrink in fear of being judged.

Well, let's move on from the heavy bits and get into something that most, if not all of you will encounter: **talking one-on-one with your professors**. As I so bravely attempted on my first day of my research methods course, engaging in face-to-face interactions with professors may be necessary for a multitude of reasons. Perhaps you simply want to introduce yourself in order to help your professor learn your name. Or maybe you, like me, are interested in connecting with your professor based on a common interest in the course material and a desire to follow in their footsteps with your future career. Communication may also be necessary due to questions you have on the material and assignments, or even to dispute a grade you received. Despite the motivation for speaking with your professor in person, it is important to remember that no matter what you bring to the table, things may or may not always go the way you had hoped or planned.

**Things can go awry for many reasons**, sometimes due simply to a clash of personalities between you and your professor, or perhaps one or both of you unintentionally bring a distasteful mood to the conversation. And, let's be honest here, we all have those days where attitudes resulting from happenings in our personal lives spill over into our educational or professional interactions. It is important for you to be aware of this within yourself and also as a possibility to come from your professor. Because, just like their students, professors have their own personal lives to live that affect their moods and attitudes within the classroom. And although you can control the energy you bring to a conversation, you cannot predict or control the same of your professor. This is a key idea to keep in mind before you decide to start a conversation, as it will help prepare you for the possibility of an alternate outcome from the one you envision going into it.

**In order to prepare for a productive and well-received conversation with your professor, be sure to first have an idea of the key points you want to bring up.** Before facing them with your question(s), it is also highly advisable to look through your class syllabus to see if any or all of your questions can be answered there. Because I promise you, if the answer is provided in the syllabus, your professor will most likely look at you with a bit of a disgustful facial expression and respond with an emotionless answer like, "Look at your syllabus." Although most of them do not say this to make you feel inept, often this response will make you feel that way just the same in the moment (take it from someone who has gotten that exact response and had to walk away like a puppy with her tail between her legs). If, after you look through your syllabus, you still feel that you need some extra clarification, then it is absolutely reasonable to approach them. Keep in mind that professors are often quite busy and may need to speak with multiple students after class, so being prompt and organized in your thoughts will maximize both your time and theirs. It is also important that you speak with your professors in a professional manner. **Although some may come across more casual than others in their communication preferences, they are still your professor and you are still their student, which calls for a certain level of respect that can easily be executed by using words such as "please" and "thank you."**

## Emailing Your Professor

Another way that you may be expected to communicate during your research methods course (and any other course for that matter) is through email. In this day and age, text messaging has become one of our prime methods of communication with others, which often includes shorthand writing techniques. It is important to keep in mind that an email is NOT the same as sending a text message and therefore should not be written as such. Instead, think of an email as an electronic version of a letter with very similar formalities. It should look something like this:

---

*Hi Dr./Professor So-And-So,*

   *Begin your email by stating your name and the class that you are inquiring about. Be sure to ask your question(s) concisely and keep the email as short and sweet as you can. When you are finished asking your questions, you may want to close out your email with something like: "Thank you, and I look forward to hearing from you soon."*
   *Sincerely,*
   *(Your name)*

---

On rarer occasions, professors may also give you an office or personal phone number to call for inquiries. If you choose to use this method to communicate your questions and/or concerns, treat it similarly to how you would speak to them in person by using clear and respectful language. Although this may seem like a weird method of contact to use with your professor, don't hesitate to use it if it is provided to you, especially if you need a quick response but feel as though your question is too complicated to provide in written form. My advanced statistics professor, for example, allowed his students to call him on his personal cell phone for this exact reason, which I found to be an incredible resource when I stumbled across complicated problems throughout the course. Remember that the communicative resources your professors provide are there for your convenience and are intended to be used, so do not be afraid to reach out to them when needed.

As we close out our discussion here on communication skills, I want to leave you with some key points that I hope you will take to heart before you approach your professor: be precise, be respectful, and above all, *be genuine*. Regardless of the formalities that you put in place to maintain a professional relationship with your professor, it is important to always be as genuine and true to yourself as possible so that they can get to know the real you. **Because YOU are worth getting to know and your thoughts ARE important.**

### Ross

Lindsay has given you some very useful and supportive advice that I hope you take to heart and use to improve your research methods experience. As a professor who has been teaching this class for many years, I would like to add some information that will help you understand and relate to your teacher even better. This should help you attain more success.

**College professors are under a lot of pressure. We have very heavy workloads and are faced with the task of trying to keep a lot of people happy. We are responsible for the education and welfare of every student that comes into our class.** It is important to us that you work hard, learn, come prepared, and keep an open mind, as well as have a good experience and maybe even some fun.

### Grades vs. Relationships

However, there are a few challenges that we run into in the classroom. By educating you about these challenges, I believe I can help you improve your relationship with your professor, for the duration of this course as well as for the future. **Remember, a grade is a short-term endeavor, but relationships can last a lifetime.** If you make good impressions on your professors, that is how you will always be remembered. However, if you make your professor's life difficult, that instead may be your legacy. When interacting with your professors, I encourage you to think about your future and not just about your immediate grade. For example, Lindsay obviously made a very positive impression on me three years ago when she took my class. I remember that she worked hard, treated me with respect, and was always honest with me. For that reason, I saw her in a more positive light, wrote letters of recommendation for her, and eventually asked her to write this book with me. If you treat your professors well, they might be able to return the favor and help you out in many ways in the future.

Let us now discuss what it feels like to be a college student and then look at how you can improve your relationships with your professors. When you first entered college, you probably had no idea what to expect because there is so much more work in college that not everyone is prepared for. This can create a lot of pressure as a student, which can in turn lead to a common approach used by many students: *seeking to get the best grade possible, with the least amount of work possible.* Although there may be some instances in which that mindset will work well enough to get by, this approach is unfortunately more likely to fail you out of your research methods class. And this is simply due to the challenging nature of the concepts and tasks you will be exposed to. Unlike other college courses you have been—or will be—exposed to, research methods does not have the same shortcuts that make the "work smarter, not harder" approach work for other classes. But, for better or worse, this class will teach you how to get things done. Perhaps not the fastest way possible, but with the necessary amount of detail and precision required for quality work. And this is a valuable lesson to be learned, as the world of research is all about delving deep into the nitty gritty. When you take this class, you should ask yourself, how can I push myself to new limits, learn new things, and conquer new challenges? That attitude will help you get through this class with the greatest success and the least number of problems.

**Students who tend to focus more on their grade and less on actually learning try to take advantage of some situations. For example, I have encountered students resorting to methods of lying, cheating, and cutting corners to try and take a "shortcut" that they thought was there to save them from the work they were required to do. Sadly, professors hear lies from students on an astonishingly regular basis.** As a professor who has truly seen it all, believe me when I say that no matter how good of a talker you think you are, we know when you are lying. The truth is, regardless of how creative you think you are, us professors have most likely already heard your same lie before … many, many times. One of the biggest problems that arises at this point is that once a student has lied to their professor, the professor will no longer feel as though they can trust their word. This could make it more difficult for your professor to believe you when you actually are telling the truth, perhaps about a grade dispute or an excuse as to why you missed the previous class and were unable to turn in your assignment. Instead, they may feel less inclined to be understanding of your dilemma. They may even begin to scrutinize or question your work more because you have set a precedent for mistruths and inaccuracy.

Now, I understand that people tell lies for various reasons, not just in ill will. Sometimes people lie because it is easier than revealing what they think may be an embarrassing truth. Perhaps that truth to a student may indicate their lack of attention and discipline, which has in turn caused them to fall behind. Whatever your situation is, your professor has also been there. Believe it or not, they were once students just like you, and since that time they have had many life experiences which you may also experience at some point yourself. If you bring something to their attention that is directly affecting your ability to focus on their class, such as the death of a loved one or starting a new or more demanding job, they may just surprise you with their willingness to understand. If you remain honest and open, you are far more likely to get what you need, such as extra time or help. It is most advantageous to focus on your relationship with your teacher rather than just your grade. We just want you to work hard and show us that you have learned the material. If you need help, come ask us. We love to help; that is why we became educators in the first place.

Apart from lying, the next most common problem I have encountered is **cheating**. The most common type of cheating is one you have no doubt already heard of -… **plagiarism**. If you have ever copied and pasted information from one source (such as a textbook or a source from the internet) into your paper, you have committed plagiarism. Some students are under the false impression that putting someone else's words under quotation marks solves this problem, but unfortunately this is an incorrect notion. Even if you put the information into quotes, it is still considered plagiarism unless the source it was pulled from is correctly cited both in the body of the text and on a references page. Don't worry too much if this information is new to you, as we will discuss proper methods of citing sources in Chapter 9.

The main thing I want to convey here is that teachers want to see that you have learned and understand the material, and the best way we can tell if this is the case is when a student is able to display their knowledge of a topic using their own words and explanations. If instead we see direct quotes copied and pasted all throughout your document, it conveys the message that you don't truly understand the material and that is why you felt the need to use the original author's words rather than your own. A good rule to live by anytime you are writing an experimental paper is to always paraphrase, meaning that you re-word any information you pull from outside sources to reflect your own personal understanding of it. In this class, you will come across many challenging concepts, so it might be tempting at times to answer questions by copying definitions from the internet or other sources. Computerized plagiarism checkers will flag these mistakes right away, and when evidence of cheating is discovered, it can have severe effects on your grade on the assignment, if not also your grade for the entire class. Plagiarism happens a LOT. As a result, teachers become tired of students not doing the work and taking shortcuts. Every teacher has a plagiarism policy in their syllabus, and if you break it, you might find yourself in the Dean's office and being removed from the college. I do not say these things to scare you, but rather to help you understand the reality of the situation so that you can make more informed decisions on how you report information in the future.

With those topics covered, I would now like to give you some hands-on practical tips for communicating with your professor. Some of these were also covered by Lindsay, which shows just how important they are. As she previously mentioned, a lot of the communication that occurs between a student and professor is done through email. Please keep in mind that most professors teach between three and eight classes and in any given term a professor may be teaching four different psychology courses. That means they interact with a lot of different students, which can make responding to emails more difficult when a student does not include certain "tracking" information that will help a professor identify which class they are inquiring about. What could have been a simple task of reading and responding to a student's question quickly becomes a task of first deciphering who and where it came from before even being able to answer the question. In order to make this process smoother for both you and your professor, try following these guidelines:

1. **Always introduce yourself with your full name as well as the course name and section (class time) you are registered in.** This

helps us put your message in the correct context and will aid in our ability to reply more quickly and thoughtfully.

2. **Write politely and in complete sentences, proofreading your letter to make sure it makes sense before you send it off to us.** Although we do not expect it to be written as precisely as one of your essays, it is still a professional document and therefore ought to be written as such.

3. **If you believe that your professor has made an error, be respectful when approaching him/her about it.** First, ask about the error and then follow up with what you think the correct answer should be and why. If your professor disagrees with you, thank him/her for correcting you and be sure to ask any follow-up questions that may help you better understand where you may have gone wrong. Again, our main concern is that you understand the material, so your ability to convey to us that you understand the reasoning behind the correct answer is very important.

4. **When pointing out a mistake your professor may have made, remember to be patient and understanding.** Professors feel a great amount of pressure to be perfect, yet they are still human and will make mistakes. If you politely point out their error, they will fix it quickly and remember your kindness.

5. **Always check the syllabus and announcements in a course before contacting your professor.** As Lindsay mentioned earlier in this chapter, professors often find it downright irritating when students ask questions that can easily be answered in the syllabus. This makes it seem as though you have not done any preparatory work before contacting them, and it can feel like a waste of time.

6. **Teachers know that they will not always be liked, but like you, they should always be respected.** If you show respect for your professor, they are more likely to show respect for you.

7. **Give your professor time to answer an email.** Please do not, for example, email your professor at midnight the night before an assignment is due and expect an answer to your question before you enter class at 8 am the next morning to turn it in. It is your responsibility to contact your professors in ample and reasonable time. Professors understand that problems will always occur while students complete an assignment; however, you cannot expect your professor to stay up late to solve your last-minute issues when an assignment comes due. Always allow your professor at least 24 hours to answer an email during the work week, and 48 hours over the weekend and on holidays.

The following offers a few example emails, including both well- and poorly written ones to help you understand the difference between what constitutes a good email and a bad one.

Example #1

---

*Professor, when is the final exam?*

Feedback: As you can see, this letter has a lot of shortcomings. It does not identify the student's name or the class/class section they are in, which will prevent the professor from being able to answer their question. Not to mention that the answer to their question is probably already in the syllabus.

---

Example #2

---

*Greetings Professor,*

*This is John Smith from your Psy 300 research methods class that meets on Fridays at 8 am. I reviewed the syllabus and noted that the final exam time that you listed there was different from the time listed on the college's website. Could you help me identify the correct time? It would be greatly appreciated.*
*Regards,*
*John Smith*

Feedback: This is a well-written letter. It identifies the student and class, points out the issue, and shows respect for everyone involved.

---

Example # 3

---

*Professor, this is Suzie Smith from research methods, why did I get a 15 out of 20 on my lab?*

Feedback: This is one of my least favorite letters because it tells me that the student put no effort into trying to answer the question on their own. Anytime a professor grades an assignment, there is usually feedback written directly on it for the student to better understand why they received the grade they did. The way Suzie worded this email makes it sound as though she did not look at the feedback already left for her.

---

Example #4

---

*Greetings Professor,*

*This is Suzie Smith from your Friday 8 am research methods class. Thank you for grading my lab. I see that I did lose some points on this assignment, but I was a little unclear on how to interpret your comments. I would like to learn from my mistakes and do better on the next lab. Can I meet with you after class or during your office hours to get some help with this?*

Feedback: This is a much better example of how Suzie could word the same question asked in Example #3. The student is polite, states her concern, and poses a practical solution to the problem. Most teachers would look forward to meeting with this student because she seems more motivated to learn and perform better in class.

Using these guidelines, emails should be relatively easy to write. As was expressed in Example #4, it is also good to keep in mind that face-to-face interactions are also a reasonable method of communicating with your professor, especially if you find that you are not quite obtaining the answer you were looking for over email. In my experience, questions get answered more quickly and accurately when they are asked in person. I realize that face-to-face communication is not always possible, like right now for example (as we are currently going through the Covid-19 pandemic). However, when it is possible to speak to your professor in person and you give it a try, you will find that your questions get answered more quickly and efficiently than over email. Now, I understand that meeting with your professor can be very intimidating. I certainly remember being fearful of some of my professors, especially as an undergraduate. However, most professors are more relaxed and friendly in their office compared to when they are in class. Therefore, meeting them one-on-one during their office hours might be a better opportunity for you to have a more positive interaction with them. It might also help you be less intimidated by them.

Now that we have discussed some methods for communicating with your professor, we are going to move on to another important topic: *preparing for your research methods class*. In the next chapter, we will talk more about what you can expect as you begin the class, as well as some of the expectations you will be faced with as you move forward throughout your term.

# 3 Preparing for Class

**Lindsay**

Before you get too far into your research methods class, it is important that you properly prepare for and understand some of the expectations for the course. Although different schools may vary in their approach to teaching research methods, there are several overlapping practices that all teachers will incorporate into their course design. We will discuss some things you can do to help prepare yourself for what is shortly to come, and hopefully this helps ease some of the looming stress you may be experiencing as you anticipate the work this class requires.

**One of the first things you may want to do after signing up for your class is to take a look at your learning management system page (i.e. Canvas, Blackboard, Moodle).** Most professors will make

DOI: 10.4324/9781003099369-3

this page available to you before your first day of class, and it will have valuable information on it that may be useful to you, especially if you have never taken a research methods class before. One of the documents that will almost always be included on your class page will be the syllabus, which outlines a lot of the necessary information for succeeding in the class. You may find it beneficial to read through your syllabus before going into class for the first time so that you are ready to ask any initial questions right off the bat. If you find that an additional question pops up later in the semester, be sure to look back at your professor's syllabus to search for the answer before asking them directly.

Before your semester begins, most professors will also use their learning management page to communicate which textbook may be required for their class. Although it is most students' approach to wait until the first day of class to get a feeling from the professor whether the textbook they say is mandatory will actually be mandatory, you may want to **consider getting your research methods textbook ahead of time and skimming through the first couple of chapters.** Especially for those of you that are going into the class already knowing that research is not your strong suit, due to either little exposure and practice in research or even a genuine lack of interest in the subject. It is okay to not be particularly interested in research methods—in fact, I think it is more common for students to dread this class than look forward to it—but regardless of your interest in the subject, all psychology majors must pass the class in order to move on to their upper division courses. So out of a necessity to at least pass the course, you may find it beneficial to spend a little extra time looking through the textbook before class begins to get a bit of a head start. Remember that once the class begins you will have other assignments and additional reading required that will take up more of your time, and this combined with work from your other classes may make it more difficult to put in the extra time you need to properly absorb the information for research methods.

Another book that you may find helpful to take a look at in your free time before classes start is your **old statistics book**, if you still have it. If you do not have your old book, spend some time looking through some of your old notes. Introductory statistics, as a prerequisite for your research methods course, is of key importance to your ability to excel in the class. A lot of the statistical tests you learned in your intro statistics course, like t-test, correlation, and ANOVA, will not only be used in research methods but also expanded upon. One of the ways in which these tests will be used in research methods that may differ from your statistics class is that you will have to learn how to use statistical software systems to run them, such as Microsoft Excel and maybe even SPSS. Using statistical software to analyze data does make it easier in some ways, such as not having to do as many hand calculations. However, it also requires you to acquire new skills, such as how to use the software properly and analyze the corresponding results tables—a topic that will be further discussed in Chapter 11. So, it is very important that you feel comfortable with how each of these tests are used, analyzed, and understood.

Along with having to learn to use and interpret statistical software systems, you will also be required to write an experimental paper, usually for the very first time. If you already know that you are not the best writer, you may want to seek out a writing tutor early on to make sure that you have someone to help you if you start to feel overwhelmed. As you will soon find out, scientific writing is very different and poses its own unique challenges compared to the writing styles taught in other disciplines. For example, when writing an experimental paper, you must be able to balance the inclusion of highly detailed information with clear and concise thoughts. EVERY fact or claim you make must be backed up by either previous research or the current research you are presenting, allowing it to be as unbiased as possible while also including your own interpretation of the information you are referencing. Don't worry if the last two sentences flew right over your head ... we will revisit these concepts and explain them further in Chapters 9 through 13. What I want you to take away from these ideas for now is that you have to be prepared for a much more challenging type of writing that will require a lot more time and attention than you may be used to, even if you already consider yourself a proficient writer. But we will get into more of that later.

If your professor has an undergraduate course assistant (UCA—sometimes called a teacher's assistant or TA) associated with your class, they may be a great resource to use **if you think you would like or need some extra help with the class**. UCAs are almost always previous students of your professor who took the same class you are taking now that excelled highly in the course. Do not be afraid to ask for help, especially from your UCA, when you feel lost. Most colleges will also have free psychology or research methods tutors if you need them. Remember that it is not only their job to successfully teach you the material and skills you will need for your upper division courses; most often they also chose that exact job because they want to help you succeed.

If in the more unfortunate case that you happen to end up in a class with a professor and/or UCA that do not provide you with the help you need, my next piece of advice would be to put in some effort to connect with at least one of the better students in your class. Now, when I say "better student," I do not necessarily mean the ones who make it blatantly obvious that they understand the topics more than you do by answering all of the questions or, in the more unfortunate case, giving off this "yeah, I know more than you do" kind of attitude. If you, like me, want absolutely nothing to do with students who feel the need to flaunt their knowledge to everyone else, then look for quieter students who you notice tend to ask more questions in class. Often the students who ask questions are the ones who, first of all, are paying attention and, second, actually care enough about the information to come up with a question that they feel that need to be answered.

If for some reason you do not feel that you will be able to work with even those students, then at least connect with someone that you feel you can genuinely get along with. Sometimes just having a fellow student to run ideas by and talk through difficult information with, or even just having someone to vent to about the upcoming assignments, will give you the support you need to get through the tougher parts of the class. Those same students may even be willing to form a study group with you, which can really come in handy before your mid-term and final examinations come around. With research methods, going it alone hardly ever works due to the bare nature of psychological research. Research requires collaboration. No matter how much of the work you think you can do all by yourself, good research requires differing ideas and perspectives. And you can't do that all by yourself.

## Note Taking

There is, however, one aspect of the class that you will have to encounter a bit more on your own, and that is note taking. Now, I won't get on too much of a soap box here, but it is important that you understand the importance of note taking when it comes to research methods. There is a lot of information that will be thrown your way during your professor's lectures … a LOT. And some of it will be almost impossible to remember the first time you hear or see it. Don't put extra stress on yourself thinking that you will remember everything your professor said during class, because odds are you won't be able to. Research methods is all about identifying and paying attention to minute details, so a good amount of the information you will be given will also be highly detailed and particular. Those are the things you will want to write down during lecture sessions.

Another piece of advice I offer you for note taking is to try to avoid feeling the need to write down everything your professor presents to you, word for word. Throughout my college career, I have always been a heavy note taker, and during my first couple of semesters I felt the need to write down just about everything from my professors' PowerPoint presentations. I thought that the way they worded it on their presentations would naturally give me all of the information I would need to understand it. Well, what I began to notice was that my professors were providing the heavily worded textbook definitions on their slides (that sometimes they would even point out sounds like utter gibberish) but would then provide a more understandable definition in their own words right after that. Even better, my professors would then give a real-life example of what they were talking about. I began to realize that instead of writing down exactly what was given on their PowerPoint presentation, I would benefit more from taking notes on what my professors said in their own words, including their examples.

**The last topic I want to touch on here is in-class attendance. I know that just about every professor on your first day of class**

gives you the speech on why their class absolutely cannot be
missed. **Although I think they all give truthful reasonings on this
point, I will strongly advocate for your research methods professor
when they give you this same speech on your first day of class. As
I mentioned before, research methods is a definition-heavy, detail-
oriented course that will require you to both learn and apply information very quickly.**
Some of you will have to absorb the information quicker than others, for
example if your school is on the quarters system rather than the semester
system. But the fact is, whether you have a 10- or 16-week term, there is
still way too much information being thrown at you in a very short period
of time. And missing class sessions makes this already stressful situation even
more stressful for your mind.

**I would recommend prioritizing your research methods class if
you can and do your best not to miss classes.** If you do need to miss a
class, be sure to let your professor know before the class session starts by
sending them a quick email. If there is an assignment due that day, do not
assume that your professor will give you an extension. It would be best to
send proof of the assignment's completion along with your email and ask
if there is anything more you can do to make sure your assignment makes
it to them on time. Before your next class session, be sure to catch up on
the notes you missed from the previous one by asking a fellow classmate
or, at the very least, looking through the chapter of your textbook that was
covered that day and write your own notes. The worst feeling as a student
is walking into class the next time and feeling completely lost because the
information given that day builds on information from the class you missed.
At that point, it may begin to feel like you have missed two class sessions,
and it only builds from there if you fail to properly catch yourself up.

## Ross

As a professor myself, I would like to throw in a few additional thoughts and
ideas to help you prepare for this class. One thing I remember from back
when I was an undergraduate student was oftentimes feeling intimidated
by some of my professors. They always seemed so aloof and stuffy, often
stuck inside their own heads too much. Because of this, I didn't find them
very approachable. However, one day as I was walking on campus, one of
my older and more intimidating professors stopped to talk with me. He
spoke to me as if we were just a couple of guys having an everyday sort of
conversation, and this shocked me. **It helped me learn that talking to
my professors outside of class, like in their office or elsewhere on
campus, was completely different than within the classroom.** Hopefully you too will come to understand and witness yourself that professors
are normal people, just like you and me. When they are in the classroom,
they are under a lot of pressure and hence present themselves in a more

formal and professional manner. Sometimes that makes them come across as authoritative and scary. But once you have a normal conversation outside of class with them, I think that your feelings about them may change, and hopefully for the better. Also, feel free to go up to the professor's desk to ask them a question if you can't make it to their office hours or find another time to meet with them. You might find that they are far more personable in that situation compared to when they are lecturing. Just be sure to have your question ready and avoid asking personal questions of your professor while in the classroom. It is best to keep the small talk to an absolute minimum in this scenario, because your professor needs to utilize the class time wisely and allow other students to speak with them as well.

**An additional piece of advice I would like to share with regards to preparing for class is to try to stay as involved and active as you are able. In other words, challenge yourself to participate. Ask questions.** Try to answer the professor's questions that he/she asks during lecture (even if you are unsure if it's the correct answer). And, as Lindsay said, communicate regularly with your classmates and group members. **If you find yourself just listening, taking notes, and turning in labs without interacting with the professor or other students, you may not be learning all that you can.** Remember why you are in school and taking this class to begin with … hopefully something along the lines of "to learn useful information to integrate into my life and future career." Even in a class that you think may be completely useless to your life or work goals, you can still learn something useful, whether it is apparent to you or not. But this can only occur if you give each class, each lecture, your full attention and effort.

Now that you are—hopefully—feeling more prepared for class, let's move on to Chapter 4, which covers difficult concepts that you are likely to encounter during your research methods course. There are several definitions and concepts that you will see at one point or another that you might find difficult to understand as you move through the class, so our hope is that this next chapter will help give you some friendlier explanations.

# 4   Difficult Concepts
##     Made Easier

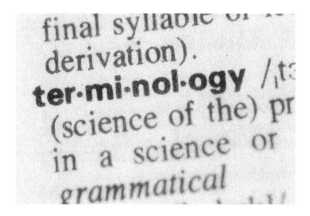

You will learn a lot of new terms in your research methods class, much like you would in any psychology class. However, there are two differences between the terms you will learn in lower-level psychology class and the ones you will learn in research methods. First, the terms in research methods are more challenging and therefore may require extra time and effort to understand. Second, you will need to immediately apply the terms you learn in research methods to the labs and experiments that you create, so it is essential that you master them. In this chapter, we have listed some of the most important and challenging concepts that you will find in your textbook. We have also provided for you the friendliest definitions and examples possible so you can better understand them.

You will be able to navigate the terms within this chapter like a dictionary, as they have all been placed in alphabetical order. That way when you come across a term that you do not understand, you can look it up more easily in midst of the many terms that will be presented in this chapter. Please note that this chapter does not include all the terms in your textbook, but rather just a set of terms that Lindsay and I have found students to find the most challenging in the past.

DOI: 10.4324/9781003099369-4

## (A)

**Alpha Level**—The alpha level, also called the p value or (statistical) significance level, demonstrates the probability/chance of rejecting the **null hypothesis** (see definition in this chapter) when the null hypothesis is true. In other words, it is the chance of a researcher drawing an incorrect conclusion based on their data and statistical testing.

For example, if you test the effectiveness of a type of psychotherapy and your research study demonstrates that your psychotherapy is highly effective in reducing depression, then you have demonstrated that psychotherapy is statistically significant. However, the big question is, what are the chances that you made an error? If you used an alpha level of .05 (or 5%), that means there is a 5% chance that the result you received in your study occurred simply by chance (it's an error) and NOT from the psychotherapy. On a positive note, it also means that there is a 95% chance that the result you received was correct and your psychotherapy did work.

Another way of looking at this is that if you were to run your experiment 100 times, at least 95 or more trials out of the 100 times that you ran the experiment would result in the same conclusion, showing that your treatment worked. However, with an alpha level of .05, there is a 5% chance that you will get a significant result, showing your psychotherapy was effective, even though it was NOT effective. Remember though that this idea can also happen reversely, in which your results indicate that the psychotherapy intervention was NOT effective when there is a 5% chance of it actually being effective.

Many researchers feel that the 5% rule (.05) is too lenient and instead use a 1% rule (.01). If you have a strong/effective treatment, a smaller alpha level can be used to provide extra confidence that your treatment really worked as it removes some of the risk that you may be supplying an ineffective treatment to people that has been wrongly labeled as a good treatment.

## (B)

**Between-Groups Design**—Also known as an "independent groups design," a between-groups design is when you have an experiment that has different participants (people) included in each of the different conditions. For example, let's say that you are conducting an experiment with two conditions, one treatment group and one control group, and you are testing the effects of Prozac (treatment) against a placebo (control) on depression (the dependent variable). In this study, each of the two conditions has DIFFERENT participants. There is one group of participants in the treatment group and a completely different group of participants in the control group. So, there might be 20 people in the treatment group and a DIFFERENT 20 people in the control group, for a total of 40 participants in all.

The opposite of a between-groups design is "within-groups design," also called a repeated measures design. In a repeated measures study, one group of participants goes through ALL treatment and control conditions. Please see **within-groups design** in this chapter for further details and examples.

## (C)

**Confidence Interval**—A confidence interval is a range of scores that most likely includes the true population mean. When we state a population mean, it is never 100% accurate as there will always be measurement error. So, if we broaden the possibilities for the mean by creating a range of scores that starts below the mean and extends to a score above the mean, it is now more likely to have the true mean contained in this range of scores.

Confidence intervals are usually stated in percentages, and a 95% confidence interval is commonly used. This means that there is only a 5% chance that our population mean does NOT fall into that range of scores. For example, if we originally state our population mean score to be 20 and we say that the 95% confidence interval is 17–23, that means there is only a 5% chance that our population mean does NOT fall between 17 and 23. In this way, it is a more accurate measure of a mean than using only a single score and leaves less of a chance for error.

**Confounding Variable**—Confounding variables (also known as extraneous variables) are any and all factors that exist outside of the controls of a research study which could influence the independent and/or dependent variables, and therefore a study's overall results. For example, if you are conducting a study on the effects of exercise on improving memory, exercise would be the independent variable and memory would be the dependent variable. However, the type of job a person has could be a confounding variable if some of the participants in your study have more physically oriented professions than others, because they may get more daily exercise naturally while at work. The amount of physical exercise that some participants get could influence both the IV and the DV in your study and thus would be considered a confounding variable. If identified, a confounding variable should be controlled or eliminated, and when neither of these options are available, then a statement in the study's results must address the issue. Reading previously published journal articles on a topic can often be helpful in learning how to identify confounding variables, especially before you begin designing and carrying out your own study.

**Construct Validity**—Construct validity is the ability for a test used to measure a dependent variable to actually measure what it claims to be measuring. In order for a test to achieve construct validity, there must be research-based evidence to validate its success and accuracy. A "construct" can be any sort of skill, mental quality, or ability, such as anxiety, intelligence, and depression. For example, if you create or use a test that measures depression, you need to show that the test you created or are currently using in your study has construct validity. One way to do that when designing a measurement scale or test for depression is to give it to a group of people and then give that same group of people other well-validated tests for depression. If your test scores correlate with the other well-validated tests, then your test has shown construct validity. At this point, however, a large number of depression scales have already been designed and have proven to display construct validity in measuring levels of depression. So, instead of attempting to "re-create the wheel," as it were, it may be the most advantageous to simply research some of the previously designed measurement scales and determine how successful they were in past studies to accurately measure depression. As long as you can provide sound evidence that the depression scale you chose to use in your study has shown construct validity with similar past studies, then the test can safely and successfully be used.

**Content Validity**—Content validity is present if you have a test that measures all aspects of the domain that it is supposed to measure. For example, many concepts, such as depression or intelligence, have multiple components to them. Depression has an affective component (e.g. feeling sad), a physical component (feelings of tension or pain), a cognitive component (thoughts of helplessness or suicide), and a behavioral component (crying). So, a test of depression would have content validity if it measured all four of these components of depression. However, if your test only measured the cognitive aspect of depression, it would lack content validity.

**Correlation Coefficient**—A correlation coefficient is a statistic that measures the strength of the relationship between two (or more) sets of scores. A correlation tells you how closely related, or unrelated, those scores are. For example, two sets of scores are highly correlated if, when given one set of numbers, you can accurately predict the other set of numbers. For example, there is some relationship between height and weight, so if you are given a person's height, you have a general idea about what their weight may be. However, since there is no relationship between age and IQ, just knowing a person's age does NOT allow you to predict their IQ.

Correlation coefficients range between −1 and +1 with a 0 in the middle. If you have a correlation coefficient of +1.0, you have a perfect positive correlation, which implies that when one group and/or variable increases, so will the other. In other words, for every score in one group that increases one unit, every score in the other variable also increases one unit. If you have a perfect positive correlation, given one set of scores you can perfectly predict the other set of scores. The same is true for a correlation of −1.0; however, in this case it would be a negative correlation and would imply that while one group's scores increase, the other group's scores will decrease. In a perfect negative correlation, if you think about it again in units, for every unit one variable increases, the other set of scores decreases one unit. Whether your correlation is a perfect positive or perfect negative, you always have perfect prediction. However, when you are studying people, you usually will never get a perfect correlation because people's behavior constantly changes. This is where the zero comes into play when interpreting correlation coefficients. The closer you are to a correlation of zero, the less a relationship exists between the two variables you are studying. Therefore, two variables correlated at a perfect zero indicates that they have no relationship to each other at all, making it impossible to draw predictions between them.

**Criterion Validity**—Criterion validity occurs if a group that scores well on a test can also perform some highly related hands-on task (criterion). For example, if a pilot enters a flight simulator and passes the simulation, the simulation has criterion validity if that pilot can now successfully fly an actual airplane. However, if in another example a person takes a written driving test at the DMV but is not able to successfully drive a car, the DMV driving test would NOT have criterion validity.

**Curvilinear Relationship**—Many of the statistical relationships that we work with in psychology are linear relationships. That means if you were to plot out one variable on the x-axis of a graph and the other variable on the y-axis of a graph and connect the two scores, they will form a straight line. For example, let's say that a linear relationship exists between height and weight. This means that as height increases, weight also continuously increases. If you were to plot out people's heights and weights and connect the dots, you would get a straight line.

However, not all relationships are that simple. For some sets of variables, as one variable increases the other variables increases at first, but then decreases after that. That type of trend would be considered a curvilinear relationship, the idea being that the two variables do not simply increase or decrease together but instead have a more complicated relationship. There are several other possibilities for a curvilinear relationship, as has been displayed in the diagrams that follow.

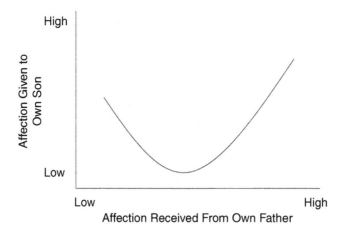

**Graph A:** As X increases, at first Y decreases and then Y increases.

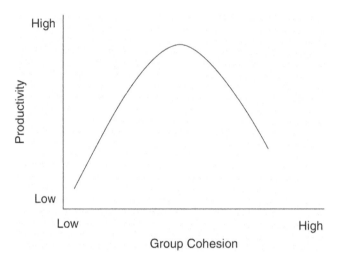

**Graph B:** As X increases, at first Y increases and then Y begins to decrease.

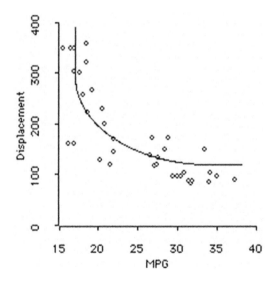

**Graph C:** As X increases, Y quickly decreases and then the decrease slows.

**(D)**

**Degrees of Freedom**—The number of scores in a distribution that are free to change/vary while still maintaining the mean of the group. Degrees of freedom for many statistics is $N - 1$, or the total number of scores in that sample minus one score. So, if you have ten scores in a sample, you can change (10 − 1), or nine of those ten scores, while still maintaining the same mean for that group. In this case, you would indicate in your results statement that there were 9 degrees of freedom.

**Dependent Variable**—See **independent variable** in this chapter for information on dependent variables.

## (E)

**Experimental Method**—The experimental method is a scientific approach in which the researcher controls and manipulates one or more independent variables and eliminates all other extraneous variables (by using random assignment and other techniques for controlling variables) to see if the dependent variable (outcome) is influenced or changed by the independent variables. **See Chapter 8 for much greater details on the experimental method.**

**External Validity**—External validity is synonymous with generalizability. An experiment has external validity if the results of the study apply to a larger population. For example, a lot of research in the late 20th century did not have external validity because it was conducted only on white, male college students and therefore could not be guaranteed to be true for the wider population, which included additional genders, races, ethnicities, and ages. If your experiment's sample does not represent the population you want the results to apply to, then you do not have external validity. External validity is achieved by using a sample that resembles the larger population for which you want your results to apply.

**Extraneous Variables**—Extraneous variables (also known as confounding variables) are variables that are present in the study but have not been measured, and thus might affect the outcome of the study. For example, if you were conducting a study to see if a man's height is related to his perceived attractiveness, the man's height would be the independent variable and his perceived attractiveness would be the dependent variable. However, what if when this experiment was conducted, some rooms had walls that were painted red and other rooms had walls that were painted white? It is possible that the color of the walls might affect the way the observers feel and hence may raise or lower the man's attractiveness score. In this case, the color of the walls would be an extraneous variable because it is present in the experiment but is not being measured or controlled. Extraneous variables should be removed or controlled when identified.

## (F)

**Face Validity**—Face validity is the extent to which a test LOOKS or appears like it measures a construct without actually necessarily measuring that construct. And if it does not necessarily measure that construct, then it is not a good measure of validity. For example, if a person takes a test that is supposed to measure their depression level and the questions appear to be measuring their depression level, then the test has face validity. Face validity alone does not prove that the test measures depression level until the test is compared to other tests of depression. If your test correlates with other tests of depression, than it has construct validity, which is a more powerful type of validity.

## (I)

**Independent Variables and Dependent Variables (including experimental and control groups, as well as participant variables)**—In an experiment, there are two main types of variables, independent variables (IVs) and dependent variables (DVs). In short, IVs are the treatment and the variables that are to be manipulated or controlled. The DV is the outcome, result, or effect from the IV/treatment. So, if you are conducting an experiment on how Prozac affects depression, Prozac is the IV (the treatment) and depression is the DV (the outcome or effect).

The term independent variable is only used for an experiment (and not a correlation). An independent variable, by definition, must be manipulated or controlled by the experimenter. What does that mean? It means that the experimenter (the person running the experiment) must have complete control over every aspect of the IV. That means that he or she can set the strength of the IV, the length of time the IV is given, what the IV is composed of, and any other characteristics of the IV. When you cannot manipulate the IV, you typically will change the overall structure of your study to a correlation.

One example of an independent variable is a textbook. If you are trying to see if a new textbook helps kids learn math better, the textbook is the IV and proficiency in math is the DV. The textbook can be manipulated by the experimenter, as the experimenter can decide what information goes into the textbook, how long the textbook is, what color the cover is, how much time the kids get to read it, etc.

Sometimes a variable looks like an IV but cannot be manipulated. Researchers call this a participant variable (PV). A participant variable is defined as a quality of an individual that cannot be (physically or ethically) manipulated. An example of a PV is a person's age, since age cannot be manipulated, controlled, or changed. For this reason, age is a PV and not an IV.

Another important fact about independent variables is that they must have a minimum of two groups (sometimes called conditions or levels). Researchers call these groups experimental and control groups. The experimental group is the group that gets the treatment. For example, if you are again testing the effects of Prozac on depression, the experimental group would be the ones to get the Prozac treatment. The control group, also known as the comparison group, does NOT get the treatment. Sometimes members of the control group get nothing at all, while other times they may get a placebo. In other cases, participants in a control group may receive the actual treatment but after the trial period is over.

At the end of the experiment, the researcher looks at how the experimental group compared to the control group in influencing the dependent variable. Ideally, the experimental group would have more of a significant effect on the dependent variable than did the control group, but sometimes this is not particularly the case.

As a final note, remember that DVs are the outcome or effect of the IVs and are therefore measured, NOT manipulated. An experiment is never allowed to alter or manipulate a DV. So, in our previous example of testing the effects of Prozac on depression, the treatment of Prozac would be manipulated and controlled while the level of a participant's depression would simply be measured and recorded.

**Interaction**—A statistical interaction is one of the most challenging concepts that you will learn in your statistics and research methods class. An interaction can occur when you use a factorial design which is commonly analyzed using a two-way ANOVA (analysis of variance) statistic.

Here is a more detailed explanation: a factorial design means that your study has more than one independent variable. For example, if we bounce off our example of the effects of Prozac on depression, we could make this a factorial design by adding in an additional IV, such as psychotherapy or exercise. For this example, we will say that the two IVs are Prozac and psychotherapy. When you run an ANOVA on your data, you will get two different types of results, MAIN effects (two of them) and an INTERAC-TION effect. A main effect simply implies how each independent variable influences your dependent variable. For example, if Prozac did significantly reduce depression, then this study would have a significant first main effect (because Prozac is the first IV). If psychotherapy was also found to reduce depression scores, then this study would have a second significant main effect (main effect of the second IV, psychotherapy). Main effects simply mean that each independent variable on its own either does or does not have a statistically significant effect on the dependent variable.

What about the interaction? An interaction is when the two factors, or IVs, work in conjunction with one another to have an effect on the DV. When we look at the main effects of this study, we see first that Prozac reduces depression and second that psychotherapy also reduces depression. So, if you gave some of the participants in your study both Prozac and psychotherapy, you would expect them to have even less depression than if you were just to give them one of the treatments. So far, we are just seeing the two main effects and not an interaction.

An interaction is when the two treatments work together to create some UNUSUAL or ATYPICAL result. So, if you were to give participants in this study both treatments and they experienced MORE depression, that would be an interaction. It would also be an interaction if both treatments made participants physically ill, since that is not an effect of either treatment on its own.

The best and easiest way to detect an interaction is to look at the graphs from the ANOVA. Most statistical software programs such as SPSS, R, and SAS should generate these graphs for you to visually evaluate. Here is how you identify an interaction in a graph: if in your graph the two lines for the main effects CROSS each other, then you have an interaction. If the two lines are parallel to each other or do NOT cross, there is no interaction. In the sample graphs provided, Graph A shows main effects with NO interaction, while Graph B shows main effects with an interaction.

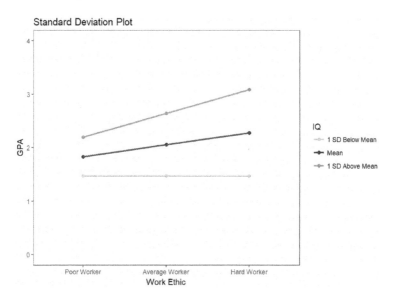

**Graph A:** No interaction because the lines do NOT cross each other.

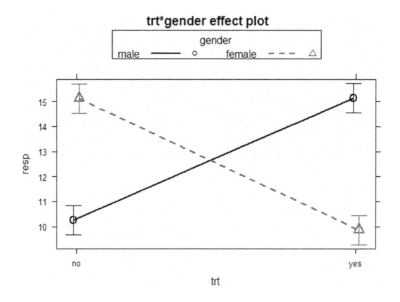

**Graph B:** Interaction exists here because the lines do cross.

**Internal Validity**—Internal validity can be thought of as another word for causation. Internal validity found in an experiment implies that the independent variable is the only variable that caused a change in the dependent variable. If a study has high internal validity, there are no extraneous or confounding variables in the study and hence ALL influences/changes to the dependent variable were caused by the independent variable and nothing else. Internal validity is an extremely important part of an experiment, so properly scanning for and eradicating confounding variables is key when designing an experiment.

**Interval Data**—Interval data uses only whole numbers, which can be either positive or negative. With interval data, there is also a ranking in which higher numbers are better (or in some cases worse) than lower numbers. For example, a temperature of 104 degrees is worse than a temperature of 99 degrees and an IQ of 140 is better than an IQ of 97. The other quality of interval scale data is that there are EQUAL INTERVALS between each number. For example, using a Fahrenheit thermometer, the difference between 98 and 99 degrees is the same as the difference between 101 and 102 degrees. So, with interval scale data, higher is better, or worse, and there are equal intervals between each number on the scale. The final aspect of an interval scale is that there is NO absolute zero. Simply put, scores either don't go all the way down to zero, or if they do go below zero, they do not completely stop at zero. Your professor may recommend that the dependent variable in your experiment be interval or ratio scale.

## (M)

**Matched Pairs Design**—A matched pairs design is an experimental design that typically includes an independent variable, a participant variable, and a dependent variable. A participant variable (PV) is a variable such as age or gender that is used in such a way that randomization is still achieved in studies of smaller sample sizes. Usually, when PVs are used alone in an experiment, randomization becomes unavailable because you cannot manipulate concrete or unchangeable aspects of a participant such as their sex, height, age, etc. However, in a matched pairs design, this becomes possible by using a PV to determine the random sampling of groups of the IV, and this is done through a two-step process. First, participants are assigned into pairs based on their scores of a particular characteristic or PV that has shown to be highly related to the DV. After our participants are matched up into pairs, they are then individually assigned randomly to the different groups of the IV that can then be tested like any other experimental design.

As an example, let's say that you are conducting a study in which you want to understand the effects of eye size and facial expression on ratings of facial attractiveness, for which past studies have indicated that larger eyes are rated as more attractive. You would first measure the size of each participant's eyes and rate their scores from highest to lowest. Then you would pair up the participants by placing the two with the highest eye measurement scores together, and then the next highest two eye measurement scores together, and so on until every participant has a pair. At this point, each of the pairs have been matched up to be relatively equivalent to one another, ensuring that each condition of the matching variable (eye measurement) has the same chance of being randomly assigned to the subsequent group conditions. The final step is then to randomly assign each individual within the matched pairs to one of the IV groups for facial expression, which could include categories such as smiling, neutral, and frowning. From there, the experiment would be tested just as any other experimental design would. Again, the matched pairs design is a good option for studies in which you would like to use a PV and/or you have a particularly small sample size.

**Measurement Scales: Nominal, Ordinal, Interval, and Ratio**— Please see these individual terms throughout this chapter.

## (N)

**Nominal Variable**—A nominal variable (or data) is a descriptive variable that indicates a name, label, or category present within the data. A **nominal variable** is one in which the data or numbers you have only NAME the variable but do not tell you anything about the quality of the data. For example, I could name three brands of cars: Ford, Chevy, and Toyota. Types of cars are nominal data because they are just names and do not denote which one is better or worse, faster or slower than the others. Another example of nominal data is the use of category colors: red, blue, white. Colors are nominal because red, blue, and white are just labels and again do not in any way indicate actual properties of the data.

Nominal data, like most kinds of data, can also be numbers, if the numbers do NOT demonstrate quality, such as better or worse or higher or lower. For example, numbers on a football jersey are nominal because although the number 52 is higher than 12, these numbers just identify a specific player and NOT whether that player is better or worse than the other players. Other examples of nominal data include peoples' names, race, ethnicity, or the style of house they live in (e.g. ranch vs. colonial).

**Null Hypothesis**—A hypothesis stating that the mean of the control group is equivalent to the mean of your treatment group. If the null hypothesis is proven true, then your treatment has no effect on your sample. If you reject the null hypothesis, you are saying that your treatment was effective and the treatment group mean is significantly different from the mean of the control group.

## (O)

**Ordinal Data**—Ordinal data, also known as ordinal variables, include data values that denote ranking order but do not necessarily have to have equal space between ranks. This could be exemplified by the use of first through third place trophies as prizes for a race. For example, John finished the race in first place with a time of 35 seconds, Mike finished the race in second place with a time of 38 seconds, and David finished the race in third place with a time of 128 seconds. Although first place is better than second place, and second place is better than third place, the time differences between first and second place (38–35 seconds = 3 seconds) is not the same difference as between second place and third place (128 seconds—38 seconds = 90 seconds). So, the first and second place runner were close in time (3 seconds difference), but third place was far behind second place (90 seconds difference).

## (Q)

**Quasi-Experiment**—A quasi-experiment is similar to a true experiment except that you CANNOT use random assignment (please see **random assignment** description next) or manipulate the independent variable. If you can manipulate the independent variable, then you can typically use random assignment and create a true experiment. However, if you are using a variable such as a participant variable, or PV (please see earlier section on independent variables), that cannot be manipulated, then you cannot use random assignment. Without random assignment, you have to use a quasi-experiment (meaning not quite an experiment). For example, if you are interested in whether men or women do better on a math test, you cannot manipulate gender and thus you cannot use random assignment. Because you are using a PV and not an IV, you then have a quasi-experiment.

## (R)

**Random Assignment**—Random assignment is when every participant in your study has an equal chance of being placed in the experimental or control group. For example, if you have a population of 100 participants and you want half of the participants to be in the experimental group and the other half to be in the control group, you would generally use random assignment. To create random assignment, you could use a computer to assign every participant a number, and then have all the odd numbered participants go into the experimental group and the even numbered participants go into the control group. You could also achieve random assignment through other means such as pulling names out of a hat or having participants draw straws with a blindfold on. Random assignment is one of the most important qualities of a true experiment and a technique that helps reduce extraneous variables.

**Ratio Data**—Ratio data (or a ratio variable) is very similar to interval data, with one big difference. Like interval data, ratio data demonstrates that higher numbers are better or worse than lower numbers and that there are also equal intervals between each number on the scale. The one difference with ratio data is that it has an absolute zero. An absolute zero means that when you reach zero on that scale, you have a complete absence of that quality. For example, zero pounds is a complete absence of weight. You cannot weigh less than zero pounds. A ratio scale must go all the way down to zero but can never go below it. Therefore, there are NO negative scores in ratio data. Examples of ratio data are height (e.g. inches or centimeters), weight (pounds or grams), and volume (ounces or milliliters). With ratio data, you can also make ratios. For example, 100 pounds is twice as heavy as 50 pounds and 6 feet is twice as tall as 3 feet. You cannot do this with interval data.

## (T)

**Type I Error**—A type I error, also known as a false positive, is when a person rejects the null hypothesis when it should have been accepted. In other words, it is when you test a treatment's effectiveness and your experiment shows that the treatment is effective. However, if your study had been done correctly, it would have shown that the treatment did not work. In the case of a clinical experiment, this would mean that the treatment was shown to be effective when it truly was not, possibly leading to individuals being prescribed a useless treatment or one that does not target the indication they are looking to treat.

   **Type II Error**—A type II error, or a false negative, is when you accept the null hypothesis and say that your treatment did NOT work, but really your treatment was effective. In a sense, you are throwing out good treatments and knowledge based on falsely invalidating results. For example, let us say that you test to see if a new textbook is better for learning than an old textbook. If the new book IS better than the old book, but your research shows that the books are essentially the same, than you have committed a type II error. Type II errors usually occur when you have a smaller sample size or your treatment is effective but not overly strong.

## (W)

**Within-Groups Design**—In a within-groups design (also known as a repeated measures design), the SAME group of participants experiences all conditions of the IV, which includes both the treatment and control groups. For example, if you have two conditions, one control/placebo group and one treatment group, one group of participants would first receive the placebo for a period of time and then the SAME group of participants would receive the actual treatment for a period of time. Each participant would act as their own control by receiving both the control condition and the treatment condition. When the experiment was complete, the researcher would look at the scores from both of the conditions to see if the treatment had a different effect on the participants than the control/placebo.

The within-groups design is a preferred technique for two reasons: it uses far fewer participants compared to the between-groups design and it has a lot less statistical error. Less error increases your chances of rejecting the null hypothesis and getting a statistically significant (successful) result from your treatment. The main challenge of the within-groups design is that it cannot be used if your treatment has carryover effects. Carry-over effects occur when one of the study's conditions has a long-lasting or even permanent effect on your participants which will affect the overall results. If you have carry-over effects, you must avoid the within-groups design and use a between-groups design. The within-groups design can also only be used in experiments in which the treatment is short-lived. You must also use counterbalancing (also known as a Latin square) to help remove order effects. Please see your textbook for more information on counterbalancing, order effects, and Latin squares.

With this information in hand, it is time to move to Chapter 5 on the topic of forming and working in small groups.

# 5 Forming and Working in Small Groups

## Ross

Research methods can be a very stressful class. I have taught it for over 25 years and I can feel the students' stress as well as my own. You may have experienced this by now or read about it in this book. So, you might be wondering, what can I do to help reduce some of this stress? **According to many of my past students, the key to a successful and less stressful class is having a good support system within the class.** In most research methods classes, there are required group assignments. These assignments may be a small part of the class, or they may be larger and more time consuming. Regardless of what is required, having good social support and peers to collaborate with and lean on can really make for a more positive experience in the class.

In the first few weeks of class, your professor will most likely ask you to form a small group of roughly four to six people. You may work with this

DOI: 10.4324/9781003099369-5

group every week of the course, including the final project. In my experience, students usually pick their groups based on who is sitting near them. **I would recommend that you DO NOT choose your group based on seating location, as it is too random and not the best way to choose a group.**

Ideally, your professor will have some sort of ice breaker or meet and greet activity early in the class. If your professor does not have one, you might want to suggest this type of activity to him/her so that you can get to know your classmates. It is very important that you find group members that you are compatible with and, more importantly, that will get the job done. Feel free to interview your classmates about their work style, their interest level for the class, their comfort level with statistics, and what type of class, work, or family responsibilities that they have. You may come up with other questions too that may help you pick good group mates.

**Evaluating your peers might seem rude, but it is a big step toward your success.** If you get stuck with a group of people that are hard to get along with or do not do the necessary work, that could make for what feels like a very long term. In my experience, there is occasionally one person in each group that ends up feeling like they do most of the work, and believe me when I say that you do not want to be that person.

Before your group is formed, there are a few other things to consider. **It is very likely that once your group is formed you will not be able to switch groups or add or remove members.** For this reason, it is important to have a group where you feel you belong. Your group may possibly have to conduct several research projects together where all group members receive the exact same grade for the assignment, regardless of their contribution. So, if you have a group member that is not doing the work, you and your other group members will have to cover for that member in order to receive the grade you desire.

Not only do most professors assign the same grade to all members in the group, many **professors might also take a "DGI"** (don't get involved) approach to group conflicts. Generally, professors do not get involved in group conflicts. The theory here is that college students are all adults that need to learn to work with diverse populations and handle conflict, as it is a life skill that is useful in additional life settings.

**Another thing to note is that most professors dislike when students complain to them about other students in their group.** It reflects badly on the person who complains as well as the person who may be slacking. Conflict always occurs in stressful environments. *How you choose to deal with that conflict will determine your success in this class.*

Here are my tips for forming and maintaining a successful work group:

1. **Pick your group carefully.** Be sure to spend some time with your group inside the classroom and maybe even outside of the classroom to see if you will work well together. Perhaps you can all meet for coffee after class one day. It is important to invest the time early in your group to make sure you are successful.

2. **Take advantage of any opportunities** that your professor gives you **to meet other students.** This will help you form your group. If there are no "meet and greet" activities provided by your professor, perhaps encourage your professor to schedule an opportunity for classmates to intermingle.

3. **Once your group is formed, accept the fact that it will not change.** Most likely, you will not be allowed to add or remove members. This is an important concept to absorb, as it will help shift your focus to use problem solving skills rather than simply asking your professor for a way out of the situation.

4. **Students will drop the class and hence leave your group.** Be prepared for up to TWO members to leave your group. Five members is a good size for a group at the start of class, although six is also acceptable. If there are more than six people in a group, some students will socially loaf or slack. Groups of four or less, on the other hand, might become overwhelming with the amount of work each student is responsible for when other members drop or if some members lack in their contributions.

5. **Always be respectful and listen** to the ideas of all members of your group, even if you disagree with them. Everyone wants and deserves to be heard and respected. If you do not like a group member's ideas, politely explain the potential flaw in their thinking and encourage the group to come up with new ideas.

6. **If tensions arise** and you cannot work it out right there, then **take a break and allow yourself to cool off.** Nobody makes good decisions during periods of high emotion. Try to avoid raising your voice to each other, learn to control your emotions, and keep your composure. Positive relationships are important for work quality.

7. **Do not complain to your professor** when there is a "problem" member in your group. Your professor might then see YOU as the problem. Do your best to work the problem out within the group. If one member continues to not do the work, work around them so that the group can still create a good final project.

8. **Focus on the WORK, not the GRADE.** Throughout my years of teaching, I have found that most students are looking for a good grade above everything else. Teachers do not care about grades. We care more about students putting effort into their work, improving their skills, and eventually taking something from the class that they can use later in life. If you frame your focus around putting in maximum effort and mastering your project, the grade will naturally come with it. Using shortcuts may be a hinderance on your overall knowledge and this may affect your grade by the end of the term.

9. **People in your group may have life issues arise** such as work, kids, and other family needs. It is important to be flexible with them but also remind them that they have a commitment to your group that must be

maintained. Your professor might even have you sign a group contract, in which case your fellow student will be held more accountable for their participation in the group.

10. **Do not rely solely on texting as a form of communicating** with your group. Text messages are by nature very impersonal and become easy for your group members to ignore. You may find it more advantageous to meet as a group in person or talk over the phone at least once a week to stay in touch and check in on each other's progress. It will also help facilitate a better relationship between all group members.

11. **Do not make personal verbal attacks on group members when you get frustrated.** That will just increase hostility and discontent. Listen and accept people's opinions and learn to calmly communicate your concerns. This is an important life skill.

12. **Let a group member's personality decide their role in the group.** For example, one person will probably emerge as a leader. If that person does a good job, let them lead. Managing a group of your peers is not an easy job. A good student leader will manage by creating positive relationships rather than bossing people around.

13. **If a group member is slacking, have the entire group meet with that person.** It is not acceptable to threaten the group member, but putting some pressure on them and telling them that the group will not cover for them may be a helpful conversation to have. Make sure everyone is on the same page in the expectation for you ALL to contribute.

14. **If a person seems to disappear or ghost you in the group, ask your professor if that person has dropped the class.** You can also ask your professor for tips on how to handle problems like this. Your professor may have useful tips on how to handle difficult students; however, do not expect your professor to intervene for you.

15. **Do not try to leave your group if you do not like them.** Your professor will almost certainly not allow you to leave your group, regardless of the issue at hand. Personality conflicts are normal and you need to learn how to deal with them. Again, it is okay to ask your professor for tips, but do not ask to be removed or name the student that you feel is causing problems. If that student is confronted by the professor, he/she might name you as the source of the problem and the professor will be less inclined to want to intervene.

16. **Start early on each task that is assigned to the group.** It is very common for many students to have poor time management skills and to wait until the last minute to complete an assignment. I have noticed that most assignments come in at the last minute. If an assignment is due in one week, meet at the start of that week to divide up the tasks. Also, create a contract that lists what tasks each student is supposed to do and you may have everyone in the group sign it if you find this helpful. Meet again in a few days to assess each other's progress. If the group is

falling behind, push each other to dedicate more time to the assignment and support each other by providing help to finish the task.

17. **If your group is working hard but continues to get stuck, tell your professor.** There are few things that annoy a professor more than getting major questions about an assignment only a few hours before it is due. Don't hesitate to debrief your professor on where you and your group mates are getting stuck and ask for help. There may just be a problem with your theory or methods, which is where your professor has expertise and very helpful tips.

18. **Never lie to your professor.** They will always know when you are lying, even if you don't think they do. Once your professor has caught you in a lie, you will lose all of your credibility. If you are truly having a problem, discuss it openly and honestly with your professor ASAP and let them decide what to do. Accept your professor's decision. If you lie, you may never catch a break for the rest of the class, even if you deserve it later on.

19. **Set up an appointment to meet with the professor at least three days before an assignment is due.** Show him/her a nearly completed and polished draft of the assignment and have him/her explain what you have done correctly and what needs to be changed. Have as many people from your group as possible at the meeting. This effort shows the professor that you care and that you have worked hard. When you present your assignment to the professor at this meeting, make sure it is in very good shape. If you show your professor junk, they will think you are not putting in the effort necessary to even be provided with help.

I hope that you have found my tips helpful in navigating through difficult group dynamics. Read on to hear more about Lindsay's thoughts and advice, as you may find it to be an additionally useful resource for your future group endeavors.

### Lindsay

Hi guys! Lindsay here again, this time with a bit of a sneak peek into my perspective on group work. After being in school for as long as many of you have, I am sure by now you have had to endure working through at least one group-oriented project in your classes. From my personal experience as a student, I have seen group dynamics almost immediately play out in one of two ways: either good group dynamics are there and everyone works relatively well together, or conflict quickly arises between group members and it turns into what feels like a living nightmare. During my time in school so far, I have experienced both scenarios, but more often than not it has ended up being the less desirable of the two options. Although I remember while in these types of predicaments feeling like I could not wait for the project to be over and done with so I could finally get away from my group members, I found later that working in these tougher group settings was where I learned the most about navigating group dynamics and how to help facilitate a healthy working environment. Not to say that my more cohesive groups weren't great learning experiences, too, because they were in other ways. But as you may have already found out as a psychology student, our minds learn best from fear, failure, and pain, all of which I think it is safe to say that we experience to some degree when working with a difficult group of students. Regardless of what kind of group you end up with in your research methods class, try to think of the experience as a tool that you can use to better navigate working in groups in the future.

I too had to work with a group in my research methods class, not only on our term-long experimental project but also during almost every class session in order to complete our lab assignments, which are a common requirement for the class. Like many of you will do, I chose the individuals that I sat next to on my first day of class because hey, at least I had something in common with them … we all made the fateful choice to sit in that very row for the remainder of the semester regardless of knowing who each other were. It's got to count for something, right? Okay, maybe not. But still, I had to believe as a psychology major that there had to have been some sort of subconscious working behind that decision. And it turned out that perhaps there was some good juju working to set me and my group members up together, because we surprisingly worked quite well with one another. Now, believe me when I say that I completely understand if you, like me, think that this is rare. A lot of groups just don't get along. That is why the process of choosing your group members and properly getting to know them is so important as you start your journey in this class.

**Usually when students are deciding who they want to have in their group, there are two different paths they take. Either they choose students they are already familiar with from previous classes or they choose the students that are sitting closest to them.** Of course, it would be wonderful if you had a perfect group of five or six friends that all worked well together to form your research group. However, since the odds of that happening are slim, we will talk more here about how to function in a group where you don't know the members well.

**In my opinion, one of the most integral moments for you during this class will be when you and your chosen group meet and talk for the first time.** It is in those first couple of minutes that all of you will be observing one another and making judgments about how things will go, just based on first impressions. Sometimes figuring out the initial group dynamic is a bit of an experiment. since each of you want to give off your best first impression. Very shortly, you will be deciding who will be taking on specific roles for the project and you will begin to recognize which of your group mates will be more likely to split up the workload evenly and provide results for assignments. This is important for you to know early on, as it will keep you ahead of the game in looking out for problems or conflicts that could occur with certain group mates.

**Things can become sticky in groups that don't know each other well, especially when there is a clash over who should be the leader. Often groups will run into the problem of either having too many strong personalities and leaders within the same group, or perhaps not having a clear leader emerge at all. These situations need to be addressed by your group to allow all of you to be able to work well together and produce the results you are hoping for.** Let's say that you tend to naturally fall into the leadership role, especially when no one else seems to be interested in the job. In this case, make sure that you are being inclusive of all of your group members and be aware if your group seems in agreement with the way you are proposing to run things and delegate tasks. You will want to make sure that while you are providing suggestions, you are also asking for and actively listening to feedback from your other group members throughout the class so that everyone can work together cohesively. **Active listening** is an important skill to engage in, as not only a leader but also a fellow group mate.

If you find that another student in your group also arises as the leadership type, it is key that you allow them to provide their thoughts and ideas just as you do. Your role within the group will occur naturally as your group mates provide their opinions about each of your ideas and decide collectively on which path they prefer to take for the project. If they together decide that your ideas are more well suited to the group's abilities and to follow your lead, then great! Lead away! But if your group mates decide that they like the other students' approach better, that is when you may find it most useful to just take a step back and allow that student's ideas to be played out.

One of the most difficult things for us natural leaders to do is allow another student to take control of a group project, especially when we feel like we could do it better. Personally, I feel the least stressed when I am in control of a situation, so that is mainly why I tend to take charge of a group when I can. My advice to you in this type of scenario is to remember to be flexible. Think about what the GROUP needs as a whole and not just what YOU need to feel comfortable. Learning how to allow others to take control is essential as you move forward both in your later classes and in your future career, simply because you will encounter situations in which you will not be allowed to take control and there are other, better qualified leaders. And at that point, it is in everyone's best interest that you be a good team player and fill the role that is needed.

Now, let's say for argument's sake that you naturally tend to fall into more of a follower role and appreciate it when another individual in your group decides to take on the leadership role. This can be a nice place to be in a group when one of its other members emerges effortlessly as the leader type and starts helping the group to organize itself. But what happens if you do not agree with how your group's leader goes about things? Or if you see them leading you and your other group mates astray? Do you find it easier to just sit in the shadows and allow that person to be confronted by your other fellow group mates? If so, know that you are not alone in your approach. Many of us do not invite this sort of confrontation openly, as it can make group dynamics awkward and tense moving forward.

It is important, though, to remember that if you choose not to speak up directly to that person about how and why you disagree with their methods, they may never be aware of it and are therefore never given the chance to better the group's experience. I can confidently say that confronting the situation is the most beneficial way to go about it, as it allows everyone to know where each other stands and can then help the group move forward without having to guess what others are thinking and feeling. As I am sure almost every relationship coach has said… "Communication is key!" As cliché as this saying has become, it really is an important one to remember when talking and working with others. When in doubt, communicate as openly as you are able with your fellow group members, and don't forget to be receptive to others' thoughts and feelings along with your own.

Along with issues revolving around the initial makeup of your group, there may be additional problems that you encounter down the road. For example, let's say that you and your group members have figured out how you will divide up the tasks necessary for your project and everyone has seemed to be understanding of their individual duties within the group. But four weeks into class, your group's literature review section is due and the two students responsible for that portion of the paper have seemed to put in close to no effort as they turn in an ill-written, two-page introduction. Meanwhile, you have spent countless hours working on your portion of the project to make sure things are done up to par for the group. Not to mention that the next week in class your group receives an upsettingly low grade on the literature review that will lower the overall grade of your project.

Absolutely… positively… infuriating. This is one all too common occurrence in group projects, where one or two students are left responsible for a chunk of a project that ends up falling short of your personal standards. A key thing to learn from this example is that it is always worth it to look over and edit each other's individual work before it is turned in for a group grade. And if the unedited work does not measure up to the expectations of the rest of the group, you can address it directly to one another and make sure that the students in charge of that particular section are being held accountable for their efforts.

**In a similar example, you may have a group member or two who fall short on their task output, but it was apparent from the moment you first met as a group that this would be the case.** All too often, there are students who, when placed in a group setting, will attempt to take a free ride through a project by riding on the backs of more dedicated group members. If you encounter a situation such as this in your research methods class, do not hesitate to bring this up to your professor.

Although in most cases they will urge you and your other group members to first confront the person directly and try to figure it out as a group, they will not just leave you and your group members to suffer through carrying that person on your backs without at least offering you some well-rounded advice. By being honest and upfront with your fellow students and professor about the group dynamics you are working with, you are inviting nothing but more opportunity for growth and to obtain help that you would otherwise not have gained by suffering in silence.

Well, now that you have heard from both Ross and myself on how to work through the various types of group dynamics that you may encounter during this class, it is time for us to move on to a bit more involved topic: *understanding journal articles*. This next chapter will be an important one for you to read, especially if you do not have much experience reviewing research or putting together a literature review.

# 6 Understanding Journal Articles

## Ross

Now that you have some good tips for creating a small group, it's time to start looking at some of the different tasks and projects that you will be completing in this class. One task that you will do many times is reading and analyzing a journal article. In fact, it's very possible that your first lab assignment will be a journal review. A journal review requires you to read a journal article and learn how and where to find the key elements such as the hypothesis, operational definitions, and conclusions.

Since almost all psychology journals are formatted in accordance with the APA Publication Manual, you will find that they not only have the same formatting but also the same general organization and elements. Throughout this chapter, we will discuss more extensively what these key elements are and where you can find them in each article that you read.

Before discussing the organization and key elements found in journal articles, I think it's more important to start you off here with a few tips on

DOI: 10.4324/9781003099369-6

how to find good quality journal articles to begin with and avoid any potential bad ones. So, where do you find good quality journal articles?

You have probably heard by now that you should always use published articles from peer-reviewed journals. What makes a "peer-reviewed" journal different from others is that the author submits the article to a journal to be published, but then the journal's editor sends the article out to a couple of reviewers. It is the job of the reviewers to read the article and decide if the article is suitable for printing. Their decisions are based on the originality of the article as well as the quality and authenticity of the article's findings. If the reviewers decide that the article is of good quality, they recommend publication to the editor. It is then up to the editor to decide if the journal should publish that researcher's article. This entire process can be quite extensive, sometimes taking as long as a full year from submission date to publication.

With the internet being the primary methods of accessing journal articles these days, there is a very popular type of research called *Open Access*, or "OA." OA research includes articles that can be downloaded and shared for free. There are two main types of OA research: OA archives or repositories and OA journals. OA archives are generally considered to be of lesser quality than OA journals because the archives are not peer reviewed. This means that anyone, and I mean ANYONE, can publish their work in these archives. The OA journals, although they are also free to the end user, are usually peer reviewed and therefore are highly preferable sources to use. When you conduct a journal search, you should always search for peer-reviewed journals, whether they come from more exclusive, private journals—many of which can be accessed for free through your school's library databases—or OA journals available online.

However, here is the big question. Just because a journal article is peer reviewed, does that make it accurate? The short and simple answer is no, not always. When you send an article to a journal to be published, the reviewers do not run your experiment again to verify the results. The reviewers take your word, to a certain degree, that your data is accurate and valid. In some unfortunate instances, honest and accurate researchers will carry out scientific research that unintentionally results in inaccurate conclusions due to errors in their methodology. In other, more dishonest instances, a researcher may purposefully tamper with or plagiarize their data and publish it in such a way that it appears to back up the claims they are making.

Regardless if, in this instance, the errors have come from a flawed research design or from tampered data, the psychology community would now be experiencing what is known as a replication crisis. A replication crisis occurs when the results from a published study are unable to be repeated in subsequent, similar studies. In other words, if you were to run these experiments again and again under the same methodology, you would not be able to get the same results as the original study. This crisis is present not just in OA research but also in reputable journals. As a result, the quality of many journal articles ends up being called into question and published research is then re-tested for accuracy. Sadly, this has occurred even with some of the most famous research done in the field of psychology, in which case the original researcher's publication is then stripped of its validity. This is why it is important that you question and remain slightly skeptical toward the research articles that you find and the conclusions they claim as truth. Use intuition and knowledge from your previous psychology classes to decide if, after reading through the different parts of an article, their conclusions actually make sense.

Now that you have a better idea of where to find better quality journal articles and how to weed out the bad ones, let's discuss the organization and structure of a journal article and where you will find all of the important parts. In your research methods class, it is very likely that you will be required to write an APA experimental paper that you will find looks very similar to the journal articles that you will be reading for class. Let's take a closer look at the major sections of an APA experimental paper and what you will usually find in each section.

Before discussing the format of an APA paper, I would like to make one important distinction between what your paper's formatting will look like, and what you may see in published articles. The formatting that you see published in journal articles may be different from the way that APA requires you to write your papers. The American Psychological Association has outlined exactly how to write and format your experimental write ups through their universally used formatting template (aka APA formatting). However, when a journal actually publishes that paper, they may make several changes to its formatting in order to make it meet their needs, such as minimizing the number of pages it takes up in the journal.

Although we will not be talking too much in this chapter about how to format your paper, it will be discussed more fully in the coming chapters. I can, however, give you a bit of a head start by advising you to start by asking your professor for APA formatting resources available to you at your institution. If that doesn't prove helpful to you, try purchasing the most current edition of the APA Publication Manual, as it provides everything you need to know to properly format an experimental paper. And if that still doesn't seem to help you, try a simple Google search and follow a formattable template, but be sure to show it to your professor or course assistant before turning it in to make sure you have the correct formatting. With all of this in mind, let's run through the key sections of an APA research article, starting at the very beginning.

## Title Page

The title page of an APA paper has several key elements, including a running head (found in the upper left-hand corner of the page), a page number (found in the upper right-hand corner of the page), a title, the names of all authors, the institution where each author works, and an author's note—which is typically information about where to find or contact the author.

If you are wondering why there is a running head, which is a brief version of the paper's full title placed in the upper left-hand corner of every page, it dates back to the years before computers. Back in the day, researchers would have to mail a print copy of their paper to the journal. Now, what would happened if the pages got dropped or the staple fell out and all of your pages got mixed up with another document? How would they know which pages belonged where? Answer: the running head! The running head identifies the name of the paper on each and every page of a document, which would allow them to be able to properly re-organize the pages. As the APA saw it, having a running head and page numbers required on every page of every document would help the receiving journals maintain the order of an author's pages and minimize the crisis that would otherwise occur with a page mix-up. Although a running head is perhaps not as important in the computer era, it is still required for this same reason.

## Abstract

Although an abstract is typically the first part of the paper that you read, it is usually the final part of the paper that is written. An abstract is a 250-word (maximum) overview that summarizes the key points of the entire experimental paper from start to finish. It is often the last portion of a paper to be written because many authors find it easier to summarize a paper after they have already written it. Sometimes an abstract is a good representation of the paper that follows, but other times it is not. When you are conducting a library search for journal articles on your topic for class, take the information you get from the abstract with a grain of salt. It is important to remember that abstracts, by nature, are extremely shortened versions of a very detailed paper. This means that they will be missing key information that may change your initial interpretation of the study. Be sure to look at the full version of the journal article before drawing conclusions based on a paper's abstract. After skimming through the actual research paper, you will either find that the abstract was a relatively accurate summary, or you will find the actual study to be very different than the abstract made it seem.

## Introduction

The introduction section, sometimes referred to as a *Literature Review* (although the literature review is only one portion of the introduction section), is the first main section of an experimental paper. In the introduction, you will encounter the following important pieces of information: the statement of the problem, the literature review, and the hypothesis.

The very beginning of the introduction section is meant to catch your attention and lure you in to read the rest of the article, sort of like a "hook" statement which you may have learned to use in previous writing classes.

I like to refer to this first part of the introduction as "the statement of the problem" because it is where a researcher indicates and explains which variables are in question, along with the reasons why the present study was conducted concerning those variables. By describing the origin of a researcher's main question, the statement of the problem helps you, the reader, understand why the article is important and how its findings will help better peoples' lives in one way or another. For example, if you were conducting research on a new treatment for depression, the statement of the problem would include information such as how many people die each year as a result of severe depression, how many days of work are missed due to depressive illness, and how much money it costs the country each year.

After stating the problem, a research article then moves into the largest part of the introduction section, which is the literature review. A literature review is a summarized review of several studies that either support or contradict the present study's hypothesis. It is important to note that a good literature review will not only mention supportive information, but also opposing research findings—when applicable—because it lessens bias within the article. It is important for a reader, especially one who is perhaps not at all familiar with past research on the topic, to be given a well-rounded overview of past research and findings because it allows them to form their own, hopefully unbiased opinion.

For example, let's say that a study is hypothesizing that Cognitive Behavioral Therapy (CBT) significantly reduces anxiety in middle-aged adults. In this case, the literature review should be filled with research that has been conducted recently on topics that similarly tested the effectiveness of CBT on reducing anxiety on mid-life stage adults. The literature review might also include broader but related topics such as the effects of CBT on anxiety in different age populations, or even gender differences in the use of CBT on anxiety. With a literature review, the more research you can acquire and include the better!

The final element included within the introduction section is the hypothesis or, in some cases, multiple hypotheses. Although having multiple hypotheses is quite common, many studies have only one hypothesis that they focus their research on. Either way, all of the hypotheses that you are studying must be stated at this point in your introduction. Hypothesis statements do not have to be incredibly complex; in fact, they usually say something to the effect of: *The present study hypothesized that CBT would significantly reduce anxiety levels in middle-aged adults*. The hypothesis(es) statements are always included at the very end of the introduction, right before moving on to the methods section.

## Methods

The methods section of a research paper is all about details and replication. Its main purpose is to give readers a step-by-step understanding of how the experiment was conducted. A methods section needs to be written with such immense detail that anyone would be able to read this section of a research article and replicate the study EXACTLY how it says. It really can't be emphasized enough how important it is for you to put in as much detail into your methods section as you possibly can for your own paper. Lack of sufficient detail will lead to an inability for your study to be repeated by future researchers. So, in the research world, all of your data and findings would be basically worthless. Remember that research findings are only considered to have validity if they are equally found in similar, subsequent studies. This can't happen if researchers down the road read your methods section and end up not having enough information to perform a follow-up study similar enough to yield the same results. We will discuss this issue more in Chapter 10 when we look at how to write a methods section, but for now let's move on to discuss each of the subsections you will find within every methods section you come across.

There are three main parts of a methods section that you will be expected to include in your paper: (1) *participants*, (2) *materials*, and (3) *procedures*. The *participants* component is usually the first subsection you will see, which will include details regarding the demographics and statistics of your study's subjects. It should provide enough detail about the study's participants to give the reader an understanding of exactly which target population the results are focused on. This information is important, first of all, to help readers understand how generalizable the research is to the larger public, but also to help future researchers either replicate or alter the study to expand on the study's results. As an example, let's say that you are reading research article about a study that was conducted which focused on the effects of an elevated high fructose corn syrup diet on attention span and focus. When you got to the *participants* portion of the methods section, you saw that there was only one statement given: *The study included 100 co-ed participants*. This level of detail (or lack thereof) provides you as a reader with just about no information as to who the research findings will be applicable to. We have not been told the participants' ages, where they were pooled from, or how many included in the study were female compared to male.

A much better example could sound something like this: *The present study was comprised of 100 total participants between the ages of 18 and 22 years old, 58 of which were male and the remaining 42 were female. The participants were randomly selected from a large community college located in Mississippi with a total population of approximately 5,000 students.* This is the type of detail that should be present in any well-written *participants* section. In addition to these core pieces of information, there should also be some information about the participants' demographic variables, such as their ethnicity, race, culture, socioeconomic status (SES), or any other variables that may be relevant to the topic. The main goal of the *participants* section is to provide readers with a detailed picture in their minds of who was included in the study, and therefore who the results refer to.

The second part of the methods section is the *materials* component. In this section, all necessary details explaining the "how" of your experiment should be listed. This would include, for example, the study's physical location and the time of day in which the study took place. You would also want to give information here on the tests, machines, tools, and apparatuses used to conduct each of the study trials, as well as any computer software programs used for statistical analysis. We call these types of details "operational definitions." An operational definition is a precise definition of any given concept or variable that explains how that concept or variable is being measured. One of the important things to remember about operational definitions is that they are subjective to a slight extent because they define particular variables as they pertain to the present study and the present study ONLY. Hypothetical constructs like emotions and feelings, for example, can have many definitions, depending on who you ask. Let's say for example that a researcher was studying "love." In order for the study to be precise enough to yield specific and viable results, he/she would clearly have to define what "love" means to THEM as well as what test they will be using in order to measure the constructs present in their operational definition of "love." Don't worry too much if that still seems a bit confusing; we will spend more time discussing how to write operational definitions later on.

For now, let's move on to talk about the final part of the methods section, which is the *Procedures* section. The procedures section is the part of your methods section that will discuss the step-by-step process of how your study was conducted. It includes everything, beginning from the researchers' very first contact with the participants and ending with the moment each participant leaves the study. This is another part of your paper that must be highly detailed because the *Procedures* section is what allows future researchers to re-run your study exactly as you conducted it. Although you are probably sick of hearing this, let's reiterate it one more time here: make sure that your entire methods section is as detailed, but precise, as you can make it. This is an essential skill to master in your research methods course, especially if you are interested in pursuing a research career in the future, because it allows for study replication and subsequent validity.

## Results

The next section you will see in an APA experimental paper is the *Results* section. I think it's fair to say that most students, and perhaps even some professionals, hardly ever look forward to reading this section because it is loaded with complicated statistics. However, understanding statistics is an integral part of being a researcher. It is in the results section that the researcher truly shows if their claims are justified. So, if a researcher states a hypothesis in their introduction that claims drug "X" reduces cancer cells, the results section is the place that they will either support or reject this hypothesis based solely on statistical findings. This is where your prerequisite introductory statistics class will come in handy, as it should have given you at least a beginner's understanding of statistical processes and language.

It is important for you as a psychology student to be able to read and comprehend statistics well so that you are able to understand just how effective, or ineffective, a given treatment is. This comes with practice—from reading and dissecting numerous results sections—and, if you so choose, taking higher-level statistics courses. Following your introductory research methods course, you will be required to take an intermediate research methods and statistics course in order to graduate with a bachelor's degree in psychology, which will teach you much more about statistics and how to report them properly in a results section. So, for now, just do the best you can and ask your professor or course assistant for help if you ever find reading or writing statistical results to be too difficult to understand.

Similar to the methods section of a paper, the results section has a few key components that are always included. They are not necessarily labeled the same as the *participants*, *materials*, and *procedures* subsections that we just discussed, but they are labeled to some extent. First, and perhaps most obviously, your results section will contain a summary including the results of all statistical tests that were run with your study's data. Now, this includes both statistically significant AND insignificant results. Both are important to report and make your readers aware of because they both answer the study's main questions. Second, a results section will typically contain tables and figures that help visually explain and illustrate the statistical results. Readers enjoy these visual aids because they help to explain the results of the statistical tests in a different, more easily digestible way. Tables and figures do have to be individually labeled and separated from the body of your results section, but we will discuss this more later on in Chapter 11 when we talk about how to properly write a results section and report statistics.

## Discussion

The final key section of an APA experimental paper that you will see is the *Discussion* section. The discussion section can be fun to both read and write because, unlike the results section that precedes it, the discussion section invites the researchers' interpretation. Because of this, it is the least structured section of the entire paper. A paper's discussion section should help explain why the results of a study are meaningful. It will usually reiterate why the study was done in the first place but also how the results can be used to help better peoples' lives and overall well-being.

The discussion section often starts by summarizing in plain language the results of the study. It also illustrates what the limitations of the study were and what (if anything) went wrong while running the study. Then it will provide the researchers' interpretation of the results and why they are valuable. The final sentences of a discussion section will usually provide ideas as to what the "next" study may look like based on the current findings.

After the discussion section, the only parts of a paper that are left are the references and appendices (if any). Every journal article cited in an APA paper must be included in the list of references so that readers are able to find and verify the information that a researcher has reported. You might find this list useful in finding similar research to the journal article you are reading, because it is a reflection of where the journal article got all of its supporting information.

With this knowledge of how to read and understand journal articles at hand, let's move on to some tips on how you can complete successful labs. Labs are an integral part of the learning experience in a research methods class, as this is where you learn to take abstract concepts and apply them to real life situations—a skill that is highly valuable as a psychological researcher.

# 7 Completing Successful Labs

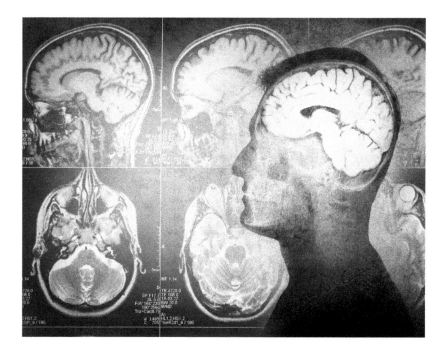

**Ross**

Taking a research methods class is very different than most other psychology classes, and you have probably already begun to experience that by now. One of the key differences that you have most likely seen is that you typically spend about half of each class period in a lab setting. It is during these lab periods when you are challenged to directly apply the concepts that you are learning in your lecture portions of the class.

In a typical undergraduate research methods class, the tasks you do during these lab sessions will be different each week, often building on the skills

DOI: 10.4324/9781003099369-7

you acquired from the prior week. In any given lab session, you might be critiquing a research article, creating a survey, designing an experiment, or analyzing data, among other things. You will also probably spend a great deal of time discussing how to write experimental papers in APA format. There are so many different tasks to learn in this course and the lab period is often where the real learning takes place.

**Although learning how to write in APA may not sound like the most exciting thing, it might be the most important skill that you will learn in this class.** As a psychology major, it is very possible that every class you take in college from here forward will require you to write in APA format. The good news about APA is that there is only one correct way to do it. So, it may seem like a burden at first, but once you finish your first paper using the correct formatting, you will have all of the information you need in order to write properly in APA for all of your other classes.

From my perspective, the main purpose of a lab assignment is to take the knowledge that you have learned in the textbook and classroom and apply it to a real-world scenario. For example, in class you will learn what an independent variable is and how it must be manipulatable by the experimenter. In lab, your professor will probably have you create a simple experiment where you must create one or two true independent variables.

If you are confused during the lab session and you are not understanding the concept you are being asked to implement, that is perfectly normal and acceptable. What is not acceptable from a professor's point of view is if you remain silent and fail to ask for help while feeling this way. Every student struggles a little, or a lot, in this class. It's a demanding class with difficult concepts that must not only be hypothetically learned but also directly applied—which is something you are not usually required to do in other, non-lab classes.

**My best piece of advice to give you with regard to your lab sessions is to do your best to become an active learner. Ask questions of your professor, communicate with your classmates, review your book and notes, and, most importantly, don't be passive when you are lost.** I know it is much easier said than done, but try not to be embarrassed about asking questions you might feel are "stupid." No questions are viewed as "stupid" by most professors—unless they can be answered simply by looking at your syllabus or additional resources previously given to you. And more often than not, there are at least five other students in your class that are thinking the exact same thing as you, and they will silently thank you for being brave enough to ask for some answers. From a professor speaking directly to you as a student, hear this: you are not a burden when you ask us for help. We are there to help you learn. This is our job, and believe it or not, we WANT you to succeed. We just cannot afford to give it to you freely without feeling confident that you are moving on from our class with the knowledge you need to further succeed in the future.

**My second tip might seem a bit obvious, but it's something that a lot of students struggle with:** *pay attention to everything the professor says and follow all of the directions given to you.* **I once heard a colleague say that 50% of a student's success in college is achieved by the student listening closely and following directions. And it is so true!** It is not uncommon for a professor to mention something only once in class and expect you to remember it. That is how we know if you are truly paying attention or not. If we give a specific instruction during class and you don't follow it when working on your lab assignment, that is one of the first things you will most likely get graded down on. So be sure to pay attention, take notes, and possibly even record the professor's lecture if he or she allows it, and always ask them for permission first before doing so.

Some people like to try to do things without reading directions, perhaps because they think they already understand what is expected of them or they like the extra challenge associated with figuring things out as they go along. Although this can be a fun way for some individuals to challenge their abilities in other aspects of life, it is NOT a good approach for college class assignments. Professors give you specific instructions because it can help you understand exactly what it is they are asking you to focus on. Think of a professor's instructions as hints as to what answer or response they are looking for. Not to mention that having specific instructions makes it easier for professors to evaluate if you are understanding the concepts. And in all honesty, it makes it simpler for them to grade your assignments and papers. When your professor reads through 50 or so papers that are supposed to be completed using the same format, they can tell who understands the concepts and who is lost. When you don't follow the professor's instructions, it takes a lot more effort for them to, first, figure out what you are trying to say and, second, decide if you are on the right track. It detracts from his/her ability to actually evaluate the quality of your work, and that alone could lower your grade on assignments.

**My third tip is one that you have heard many times already in earlier chapters: be detailed. Research methods assignments are all about the details.** You cannot have too many details in your assignments. Research is dominantly a left-hemispheric way of thinking that focuses largely on language, numbers, and precision. There is not much creativity needed when conducting a psychological research study apart from when you are initially designing it. Even then, a lot of what you are doing is replicating what others have already researched, sometimes with an added element that will add to that research. And as I have said before, the only way to replicate a study properly is for it to be written precisely with a LOT of details.

For example, if your professor asks you to perform a task that sounds simple, such as to describe what your pencil looks like, there are still both good and bad ways to do it:

BAD: *I have a yellow "Jones" brand pencil.*

BETTER: *I have a yellow "Jones" brand pencil with a graphite tip and a red eraser.*

BEST: *I have a yellow "Jones" brand pencil that is 8 inches in length and ½ inches in diameter, with a fresh red eraser, never used, that is ½ inches in length and ¼ inches in circumference. The pencil appears new with minimal previous sharpening. It is close to its original length of 8.5 inches. When it is used to write with, it creates a straight thin line that is even, sharp, and narrow, displaying the correct precision.*

Now, this last example may seem strongly over-detailed and overdone, but this is the type of information that is highly valuable in research. Research is all about replication, and replication is all about precision and details.

**My fourth tip to completing successful labs is another somewhat obvious one: read your assigned chapters before you come to class.** Your professor will probably lecture on the topics covered in the textbook they require with their course; however, if you read the chapters in advance, you will know what concepts you understand and which concepts leave you confused. Reading ahead will allow you to ask questions about difficult concepts during the lecture as they come up instead of later on while doing an assignment and having to find other, less direct ways of finding the clarity you need. Remember, if you don't understand a concept, many other people probably don't understand it either and you will all benefit from bringing it up in class.

**Another thing I urge you to do is ask your professor if they are willing to read rough drafts of your labs and other assignments before you turn them in.** Every professor has their own rule about this, as it does take a lot of time out of their schedule. I find that motivated students will send me their labs well ahead of the due date if I promise to give them some feedback on their work before I officially grade it. That way the student can revise their work before turning it in for a grade. My feedback is meant to help my students digest the material correctly, and it usually helps them get a higher grade. I allow students to turn in only one rough draft per assignment as it is a very time-consuming process for both the student as well as myself. However, I believe that it leads to greater knowledge and success for my students, so it is worth it. Hopefully you will find that your professor, like me, finds this same value in allowing you to bring in assignments early to obtain some constructive feedback. If they do, take advantage of this to maximize the outcome of your work.

**One last tip I would like to give you is this: it is absolutely acceptable to ask your professor for more time on an assignment**

**on occasion, but you must ask for the extension well before the assignment is due.** If you truly feel like you need more time to turn in a well-produced assignment, you must be able to show your professor that you have already put a lot of effort into the assignment. For example, let's say you are working on your lab in class and the professor only makes themselves available until 5 pm, but the lab is due at midnight. If you have been working hard but are unable to finish the assignment before your professor leaves, show them what you have accomplished by five o'clock and then ask him/her if you can have a few more hours, such as until noon the next day. Chances are your professor does not begin grading assignments the moment they are turned in. So, if you have a just cause for asking them for extra time, that may be acceptable. But keep in mind that some professors are stricter with deadlines than others, so do not expect them to allow this kind of extension on your first try. For professors such as myself who do occasionally allow extensions such as these, the bottom line is that we would much rather grade a good paper that is a little late compared to a bad paper turned in on time. Whatever you do, refrain from emailing your professor just before, or after, the midnight deadline asking for more time. This not only makes you look lazy, but also irresponsible and disrespectful of your professor's time.

Those are my six big tips for you on completing successful lab assignments; however, I do have a few additional, smaller tips that I would like to briefly mention. First, always make sure you use the word processing program mentioned in the syllabus. If your professor asks you to use Microsoft Word, it's probably because his work computer or learning management software won't open other programs like Adobe (PDF) or Apple (Pages). Second, write carefully. Be sure to organize your thoughts clearly using paragraphs with indents, proper spelling, and complete sentences. I can't tell you how many students have asked me in college classes, *do spelling, grammar, and punctuation count toward my grade?* Yes. This is college … they always count. No professor, or you for that matter, wants to read a poorly written paper. Lindsay will attest to this fact, as she was asked to read stacks of student papers as an undergraduate course assistant and for the first time, I think she fully understood the difference it makes to read a well-written paper vs. a poor one.

**One more thing: APA formatting is extremely important. Always write in third person and past tense, using *Times New Roman*, 12-point font. You also want to make sure that your document has 1-inch margins that is written double spaced with one space between each sentence. If you are new to APA formatting, my advice is to take some time to read the APA publication manual, as much of it can be found online. Once you learn APA, you can use it for the rest of your educational career.**

With those recommendations in mind, I will now turn things over to Lindsay so she can give you some student-centered tips on completing your lab assignments.

# Lindsay

As a post-research methods student who is now writing a book about research methods, I have found myself thinking back to my own experiences as a student fresh to the world of research. Back when I was standing directly in the shoes you are in now, most likely taking your first research-based class in your entire schooling career. I can close my eyes and still see a clear picture of my classroom with my group mates sitting beside me, and Professor Seligman (as I knew him back then) presenting his lecture while I critically wrote down my notes. I also remember the lab sessions that my class had every Friday, and how different those were from anything I had known before. For the first time, I was not being asked to simply participate in a PowerPoint lecture. Instead, I was being asked to work collectively with my peers to complete what seemed to me like mini projects. Although I found this to be quite refreshing, I also realized that I was completely unprepared for how independent my group and I were asked to be with these projects. Professor Seligman would talk only for about ten minutes to offer directions for the lab project assigned that day, and then we would be on our own and have to look to each other and our notes on the topic to somehow complete what was probably the lengthiest in-class assignments that I had ever faced.

If your class is anything like mine was, you may soon feel a similar way when you get to your first couple of lab sessions. For that reason, I would like to offer you some of my retrospective thoughts on the lab assignments that I had to work through, in the hopes that you are able to gain some useful insight that you can use to your own advantage. Especially as you get further into your term and are required to do tougher, more lengthy projects in the same short amount of time.

One important component of successfully completing lab assignments is being able to look back at relevant information, whether that is your lecture notes, the professor's slide deck, or your textbook. That being said, it is necessary for you to have at least one of these resources available to you during your lab sessions. I would advise that you bring your own resources, even if one or more of your group mates say they will bring theirs for your whole group. I say this because there is nothing more frustrating than relying on someone else and being let down. They could simply forget to bring their textbook or notes that day, or perhaps they do bring their notes but they are illegible or confusing to you. No matter what the case may be, you are pretty much out of luck at that point and have made your lab assignment for the day significantly more difficult. To avoid this unfortunate circumstance, I highly suggest bringing your own materials so that you have all of the information you need and do not have to rely too heavily on others.

**Once given your lab assignment instructions, it is then up to you how you will tackle the project. You will get to decide how to organize your time according to the tasks you are presented with.**

**This is where your time management skills will be tested, and it is very important that you keep track of time in your head as you move along through the assignment.** It can become easy to get lost in one of the tasks once you get going, so be sure to maintain awareness of how much time has gone by and how much time remains. If at any point you start to feel like you are spending too much time on single parts of a lab project and may not finish, it is then perhaps time to change your approach. For example, instead of finishing each portion of the assignment one at a time like a checklist, you may try getting each one partially done and then going back through each part a second time to finetune your work. That way, if you run out of time, at least you have partial work done for all portions of the assignment instead of just having two or three full portions done out of five or six (or however many parts to the assignment there are). This is only one example of many time management techniques you can implement during lab sessions, so feel free to experiment with other techniques as well until you find one that works best for you and your working preferences.

Most professors will ask you to complete lab assignments using APA formatting (or perhaps BPS). If so, the last thing you should do before submitting your work is checking your document to follow proper formatting guidelines. If you are asked to use APA formatting, you would want to make sure your writing is double spaced and 12-point, Times New Roman font. It is also a good idea to re-read your entire document to edit for any spelling, punctuation, and grammar errors that you may have missed while initially producing your responses. Although it may seem like these small errors are unimportant, this is definitely not the case. Most professors I have spoken with about this issue say that papers with incorrect spelling and grammar make it difficult for them to focus on the actual content of the paper, which usually leads to a lesser understanding of the student's point. And this naturally then leads to the student getting a much lower overall grade than they probably would have if their writing was more understandable. That said, it is certainly worth the few minutes of your time it takes to read through your finished document one last time.

All of the skills that Ross and I have touched on in this chapter are extremely useful in other areas of your research methods class as well, such as for your final experiment project. Your lab assignments, if designed well by your professor, will naturally prepare you for the type of tasks you will have to perform for your experimental project. So, the more you practice your time management and writing skills during your lab sessions, the better off you will be. Let's move on now to talk more about how to design your final project.

# 8 Designing Your Final Research Project

The most important part of a research methods class is designing a research experiment, carrying it out, analyzing the data, and writing up the final experimental paper. The second half of this book will focus on this project and how to do it successfully. This chapter will focus on the first step: designing your experiment. A research study is a big project that will most likely take more than half of the term to complete. You will be working either in a small group or perhaps by yourself, depending on the class size and the college's requirements. If you are working in a small group, please review Chapter 5 for some helpful tips.

**Your first two steps will be to decide what your topic or hypothesis will be and what type of research project you will conduct (e.g. experiment, survey, observation, etc.).** The type of research study that

DOI: 10.4324/9781003099369-8

you do may be largely controlled by your professor, but the topic will be entirely up to you. Many research methods professors require their students to do either a laboratory or field experiment since it's a more challenging project than a simple correlational study. Later in this chapter, we will discuss more about how to create an experiment and some of the key elements of an experiment.

**Before you start your research project, you should check the syllabus and any documents that your professor has provided for you to help you design this experiment.** Chances are that your professor has some idea of what he/she wants to see in this project. If you don't have any course documents about the requirements for the final research project, be sure to ask your professor near the start of the term. He/she will probably start to discuss this topic during the first few weeks of class.

When it comes to designing a research study, there are several different types of research projects to choose from, including archival data, observations, survey projects, and experiments. Make sure that your professor will allow you to do the type of study that you are interested in before you begin; otherwise, you may have to start from the beginning and re-design your entire study.

**Regardless of the type of research project that you settle upon, one of the things you will be told early in the class is that you must do a research project that is *ethical*. From your professor's perspective, unethical studies are not just the outlandish-sounding ones that include shocking people or causing them pain or harm. Even the most seemingly harmless of studies can be carried out unethically, and therefore you should always run your ideas of how to design your project by your professor.** Chances are that he/she will want you to do something simple, clean, and, most importantly, non-offensive. Quite often a student will want to do an exciting project that will naturally make some waves at the college. However, if this is your first research methods course, the purpose of this project is not so much to create new knowledge and get published as it is just to learn how to do research. Some students request to do topics on things like breast feeding, inducing stress, or using coercive techniques because they have read about these types of studies in their other psychology classes. Keep in mind that the APA ethics code is a lot stricter than it used to be and many studies that you might have read about in your introduction to psychology class have now been banned. Before starting a research study, ask yourself if you or your classmates would agree to participate. If the answer is no, it is time to come up with a new idea.

With all of these restrictions placed on what you can do, what are some possible research topics that can be done in a short amount of time that don't create unnecessary controversy, yet are still good topics? There are lots of simple yet fun topics out there that you can explore as your first research experiment. For example, you can create a simple intervention to help people learn better or improve their memory. You can teach people how to meditate or relax and then test their anxiety levels. You can also go out into your college's quad and sit right next to someone and see how they behave. You can walk by strangers while smiling and waving to see how they respond. Sometimes you can even carry out a slightly atypical behavior like walking through the quad on a snowy day, wearing a t-shirt and shorts and have a classmate observe people's reactions. As you can see, a research study can still be fun without being offensive or unethical.

**Once you have some basic ideas for your hypothesis and experiment, you need to make a few decisions. Are you going to work with humans or animals? Will you work in a laboratory, classroom, or out in the field? Can you do your study online? Must it be an experiment, or can it be an archival study, observation, or survey?** How much time do you have to carry out the study? These are all integral questions that you must be able to answer in order to properly plan out your project. You might only have a couple of weeks to run your study from start to finish, so plan carefully and make sure that the project doesn't get to be too large. Your professor should give you guidance on all of these questions, but if you feel like you need extra help on answering all of these, be sure to ask them.

As we mentioned at the start of this chapter, many research methods professors require their students to do experiments rather than correlations or observational studies. This is because an experiment is a much more complex project compared to the others, and professors want their students to understand what it really means to *manipulate* an independent variable. Because many students struggle with the concept of what a true independent variable is (as opposed to a participant variable), it is important to spend a little time here on this topic. For a research study to be a true experiment, the study must have two elements: (1) an independent variable that is completely manipulated and controlled by the researcher, and (2) the experiment must use random assignment. Let's first take a look at what a manipulable independent variable looks like.

A true independent variable is one that the researcher can create, change, or modify in any way that they want. For example, if a researcher is testing out a new book in the classroom, the new book can be created or manipulated to reflect what the researcher is trying to accomplish. The researcher can determine, for example, what pages or information go into that book, how long the book is, which students or classes get the book, what color the book is, and anything else that they deem important. Another example of a variable that can be manipulated is a new medication. The researcher can determine what is in the medication, how much medication the participants get, how many participants get the medication, how many do not get it, etc. The researcher can manipulate any aspect of the medication that they wish (with some limitations on the composition of the drug), and therefore it is considered an independent variable.

Independent variables are often treatments or interventions such as Cognitive Behavioral Therapy (CBT) or an Anger Management Training session. For each of these variables, the researcher can define what the therapy sessions will look like, how long they will last, how many people get them, and so on.

As a contrast, let's take a quick look at variables that CANNOT be manipulated and hence CANNOT be an independent variable in an experiment. For example, you cannot manipulate or change a person's age, gender, or race. There are also other variables that can be physically changed, but it is considered unethical to do so. Self-esteem would be an example of this type of variable. It is possible to lower a person's self-esteem, but it is generally considered to be unethical because it can cause severe damage to an individual's mental health and well-being. Variables that cannot be manipulated physically or ethically cannot be independent variables in an experiment. They can, however, be used in other types of experiments like correlations and quasi-experiments.

The first test to see if you can run a true experiment is to make sure that you have at least one independent variable that you can completely control. The second thing you must do is make sure that you can use random assignment with your study's participants. Random assignment means that every participant in your study has an equal chance to be in all of the possible groups. Imagine that you are running an experiment and you have brought 100 participants into the room. Your plan is to get 50 people assigned to the experimental group while the remaining 50 people are assigned to the control group. To do this, you must randomly assign each of those 100 people a number. You can accomplish this by having them each draw a number out of a hat or even by using a randomized number generator. Then you must have a method of equally splitting them into each respective group. For example, you could place every participant who is assigned an odd number into group 1 (the experimental group) while those given an even number will be placed in group 2 (the control group).

**Now that you have created your groups using random assignment, it's time to introduce your independent variable, or treatment, to your experimental group.** Remember that the independent variable is something that you *introduce to the participants from the outside*. It cannot be something that the participants are already exposed to, as we noted earlier in this chapter. The IV must be brought in and given to those only in the experimental condition. Variables such as age, gender, self-esteem, or even mental illness or alcoholism CANNOT be used as independent variables because they are pre-existing qualities of a participant and cannot be physically or ethically manipulated. In short … if the variable can be manipulated, you have an experiment. If the variable cannot be manipulated, you have a correlation. It's that simple! Where this gets minorly complicated is with *quasi-experiments*, which are a sort of middle-ground type of study with requirements that lie in between a true experiment and a correlational study. Your professor might discuss quasi-experiments more with you than we will here, and if they do, they may even allow you to run one as your term project. Before doing so, be sure to still discuss your ideas with your professor before you begin running participants.

Now, once you have determined what type of study you will be running, you will then want to think about how many independent, dependent, and confounding variables you will look at. You really want to work with your professor on this, because adding a variable can change the statistics used and possibly make your experiment a lot more extensive than you will have time to complete. In my opinion, you don't want to have more than two independent variables and one dependent variable per experiment. You may also want to limit the number of extraneous or confounding variables you examine to only one or two. If you were running a full-blown experiment intended for publication, you would examine all possible confounding variables. But because the purpose of this assignment is to simply teach you the basics of *how* to run a study, it is unnecessary for you to make it extra complicated on your first try. Your professor may not even require you to include a confounding variable at all; as a matter of fact, oftentimes the confounding variables are nothing more than participant demographics.

As you have seen, there is a lot to think about when you are creating your own experiment. I'm going to wrap this chapter up with a few smaller topics. One thing I always like to tell my students is that you need to remain open to change. For example, when you come up with your study's topic, it is always good to have a couple of back-up choices just in case it doesn't pan out the way you hope. It's very possible that your professor will turn away your initial idea because he/she already knows that there is no research on the topic, or that the experiment won't work or the topics are too broad and poorly defined. This is all part of the process, so be open to new ideas as you go along.

Your professor might approve your topic, but after you start looking for research for your introduction, you may find that there is not a lot of research on that topic. At that time, you might want to present a different topic with new variables to your professor. Your professor generally will not mind if you switch topics for good reason, but sooner in the process is always better than later. It's generally also acceptable to replicate a study that has already been published. Remember that your job is simply to learn how to do research, and this does not necessarily mean that you have to create new knowledge.

**The final topic to discuss in regard to creating your experiment is where and how you should find the participants for your study.** This of course is a very important aspect of your experiment, as it will be at the cornerstone of your study's generalizable findings. Some colleges may require you to include only students enrolled at that college. Others might allow you to find participants from your greater community, or people found through online sources such as social media. Most colleges will have strict rules on where you get your participants, so be sure to clear it with your professor before gathering participants for your study.

**For example, when I (Ross) teach my research methods class, I only allow my students to use participants that can be found on campus.** Chances are that your professor will tell you something similar. Many colleges require this because of liability. If there are any complaints from the participants, they want to keep them on campus, rather than have them spread through the community. The school doesn't want to be sued. The bottom line is that for your first experiment, it really doesn't matter *how* you gather your participants. A convenience sample will be fine since the nature of your study is to learn how to conduct research, not to necessarily to get published.

To help you recruit students from other psychology classes, some schools will use software programs that makes it easy for researchers to connect with students that may be getting extra credit to participate in your study. Keep in mind that you can also recruit a special population found at the college if it is relevant to your study. For example, specialized groups on campus such as the football team, veterans' center, chess club, or the LGBTQ+ community might be very interesting to study depending on the nature of your research. As long as you have your professor's permission, of course. It is always a good idea to get written permission from your professor before you target a specific group, as it keeps you and your participants safe if any questions come up from your college. *Never pick a topic, conduct a study, or change your topic or study without your professor's permission.* He/she is there to help you. Your professor will help to guide you toward a topic that will work for your experiment and won't cause harm or unnecessary controversy to your participants or the greater student body.

With those thoughts in mind, it's now time to start talking about how to write your experimental paper. We will start off by discussing how to write a literature review. Then we will discuss the methods section and how to create an effective research methodology for your study. As we discuss the methods section, we will also talk about how to find participants for your study, what constitutes a good sample, and some experimental designs to consider.

# 9 Writing an Introduction/ Literature Review and Reference Page

## Narrowing Your Topic

The first large section of your paper is the introduction, often called a litera-ture review. To write a literature review, you need to have a focused topic followed by lots of scholarly research on that topic. Let's say for example your topic is: *How does listening to classical music improve explicit memory reten-tion?* This topic has two variables, classical music (IV) and explicit memory retention (DV), and is a good example of a narrow, focused research idea.

Notice how that topic compares to this one: *What are the effects of music on memory?* This second topic is comparatively vague and would therefore be hard to research. This is mainly because there are many different genres of music and multiple ways to classify memory. If you were to go to a database and search the keywords *music* and *memory*, you would end up drowning in articles that may or may not be relevant to what you are actually looking for.

DOI: 10.4324/9781003099369-9

## Finding Articles

Once you have your topic narrowed down, you can begin to search databases for scholarly research. A few tips about your search: first and foremost, **never do a Google search. Not even a Google scholar search.** Also, try to avoid an open access journal article search. The problem with these sources is that they often include research from parties who agree to pay to be put up on that given database. This increases the likelihood of you stumbling across biased or invalid research articles that, if they had been sent to a credible journal, would most likely have been rejected. A researcher such as yourself should only search databases of peer-reviewed, scholarly psychological research. No internet sources, magazine articles, or newspapers should be used to support your topic. Use your college library's psychology databases and use the most specific terms you can, such as *classical* music and *explicit* memory retention. It is also important that you use articles that are current, ideally within the last five to ten years. It is best to avoid using classic (old) research unless it's just one article to introduce the topic.

If you have trouble finding articles, it's usually because you may not be familiar with the correct search terms to use. Sometimes finding the right search terms is achieved through trial and error, and sometimes it will require the help of your professor. If you find yourself searching term after term and it's not bringing up quality research on the topic, seek the help of your professor. A lot of times a more experienced researcher knows what terms will work and what terms will not.

As you come across journal articles that you would like to use, be sure that the full text is available for download before deciding to use it. On most database sites, there is a way to filter your search results to include only full-text articles. For your literature review, a significant number of articles are required. Your professor will most likely tell you how many articles that you need for this section, but a good rule to follow is to have at least ten to reference. It is a good idea to find more articles than your professor suggests because after you read those articles carefully, you may find that some of them don't quite work for your paper and may have to be thrown out.

## Read More Than Just the Abstract

Another important tip for gathering research is to read the actual article, not just its abstract. Many students—and even teachers—gather stacks of articles that they feel are relevant for their paper based only on the abstract but end up being sorely disappointed later on when they go to read the full article. The problem is that an abstract is an extremely summarized version of a very detailed experiment and therefore does not always accurately represent the full article.

## Organizing Your Articles

Once you have found at least ten or more good articles, the next step is to organize those articles into the order that you will be using them in your paper. There are a few ways you can organize your journal articles. One way is to make one pile for the articles that discuss your independent variable, another pile for those that discuss your dependent variable, and a third pile for articles that cover both your independent and dependent variables together. You might want to divide the third pile into two more piles, one for articles supporting your hypothesis and the other for articles that contradict your hypothesis.

After organizing your articles, it is then helpful to write summaries for each article. Summarizing one article can be a bit of a time-consuming task, easily taking 30–60 minutes. However, they will be extremely useful when you begin writing your experimental paper and need to reference each of your studies. Writing a summary is similar to writing an annotated bibliography, as your goal is to report the main results of each article. When you are summarizing, you can also add in some critiques of the article. Even an article that supports your hypothesis may still have some flaws that you want to point out. For instance, you can say that although the article supported the hypothesis, it did have a small sample size that may have affected the results. Then, when you plan your own experiment later on, you will be able to address some of the flaws you found in previous studies to improve the overall quality of your study.

**As a general rule, try not to write more than four or five sentences for each article summary.** Although it may sound simple, summarizing effectively is a task that many students struggle with. When asked to write a one-paragraph summary of a 12-page research article, you are being asked to condense highly detailed information into one main idea. In other words, you are being asked to zoom out and see the bigger picture of what the researchers are trying to convey. This type of writing takes practice, but it is a valuable skill that you may learn to really appreciate later on.

It is also very important that you reference each of your articles correctly in APA or BPS format. One of the mistakes that students regularly make in their literature review is with in-text citations and their corresponding references at the end of the paper. All you need to do to get started with this is to simply look up online or in a publication manual for your corresponding formatting style how to reference an article (or other source). Make sure to use the correct punctuation, capitalization, and italics where needed. When students fail to reference an article in the correct format, professors will usually grade down for this and it becomes an easy way to lose points on even a well-written literature review.

Another instance in which you will significantly lower your own grade in this section of your paper is plagiarism, one of the most common problems found by professors in student writing. **Plagiarism is a big issue, as students don't always realize when they have committed it. A foolproof way to avoid plagiarism is to always paraphrase, meaning always put information into your *own words*. Avoid copying and pasting passages from an article and placing it directly into your paper, even under quotation marks.** Some professors will allow you to include some direct quotes in your paper as long as they are cited correctly. However, most professors dislike direct quotes as they make it seem like the student did not truly understand what the author was trying to convey. A student's ability to paraphrase a complex sentence from a scholarly journal article shows a much deeper level of understanding than pulling direct quotes from an article and is therefore much more desirable.

**Another way to avoid plagiarism is to include a reference for *every fact* that you include in your paper. As researchers, we never assume that any information is common sense, even if it may seem that way to you personally.** All of the information we report must be backed by evidence, so you must have a scientific reference for all of your claims in your paper. For example, a student may report what seems to them like basic psychological concepts which they learned in their introductory psychology course and therefore do not feel the need to cite it. Unfortunately, this too counts as plagiarism. In order to include this information in your paper, you would have to cite a proper source such as a previous textbook or research article that provides evidence of what you are claiming to be fact. As another example, a student may successfully describe in their own words what a given study found, but then forget to include an in-text citation and/or reference for it. Although this may be an honest accident, it is still considered plagiarism since the original author was not given proper credit for their work, and this can have the same consequences as any other act of plagiarism.

With the uncomfortable topic of plagiarism out of the way, let's move on to discuss how to actually write your literature review. The first thing you may want to do is read the literature reviews from each of the articles that you have found. Those, along with any examples of well-written literature reviews that your professor provided to you, will prepare you to write a good one on your own. From there, it is all about good preparation and planning. Reading lots of good reviews will naturally help you prepare, but openly thinking about and visually brainstorming some ideas of what you want to write will also help. Writing a detailed outline is perhaps the best ways to create a foundation for this section of your paper because you can use it as an organizational guide while writing, instead of having to piece together information as you go along. You might even want to show the outline to your professor before you write the full literature review so they can give you some constructive feedback that could save you some time.

When you go to write your literature review (not necessarily the outline) you should also include APA subject headers to help organize your paper.

Be sure to look up the different levels of APA subject headers before you create them. You should start your literature review with the introduction. The first header will look like this in your paper:

## Introduction

*★Notice that the header is centered, capitalized, and in boldface text.*

In the introduction, I generally like to start out with what I call "the statement of the problem." The *problem* is your dependent variable. I like to call it the *problem* because your DV is often something that needs to be improved on or fixed. It is very important that you focus on your DV here and not your IV.

For example, let's say your research study is on the topic *how to decrease depression with Cognitive Behavioral Therapy (CBT)*. In this case, your IV would be *therapy* and your DV (aka "the problem") would be *depression*. When you start to create your statement of the problem, you will need to come up with an eye-catching statement that is backed up with at least two research studies, which you will include as references. The purpose of this statement is to entice the reader into reading further, and this only occurs by making them interested in your topic. Think of it as the equivalent to a newspaper headline. You have to sell your article based on that initial opening sentence. In fact, most researchers will only read the first sentence of your article before making a decision of whether or not they want to finish reading it or move on to another article. An example of a statement of the problem for this topic might look like this.

> *Depression is a pandemic in our society and leads to over $10 billion in lost work time, disability, and even death, each year.*
> (Author Last Name, 2018; Second Author Last Name, 2020)

Once you have finished this opening statement, your next feat is to complete the rest of the introduction section of your literature review. The introduction is simply an elaboration of the research on your DV and it is your goal to convince the reader as to why we need to study it further. If the reader gets through the introduction and believes that what you are studying is in fact a real problem that needs to be addressed, you have done your job.

Once the introduction is complete, I like to then focus on independent variables—other than the one you are looking at in your study—that have been used to study that same dependent variable in the past. In our current example, you might look at treatments apart from CBT that have been used in research studies to improve depression in participants. Your section might look like this, beginning with a *level-2 subject header.*

**Treatments for Depression**

Note that your level-2 header is flush left and in bold. In this section, you might talk about other treatments for depression, excluding Cognitive Behavioral Therapy (CBT). You can discuss other types of psychotherapy or even drug therapies that have effectively or ineffectively been used to treat depression. Be sure to reference every fact you use from the articles that you find. There should be a good number of relevant facts and references included in this section.

Once you have completed your introduction, you will then move on to the more focused part of the literature review where you examine research on your specific topic. In this section, you only discuss the research on your two variables. In this case, it would be *CBT* and *depression*.

Your next level-2 header and section might look like this:

**Cognitive Behavioral Therapy and Depression**

This section will be the bulk of your literature review and will focus only on those articles that discuss your specific hypothesis of how CBT improves depression. This section is going to have a paragraph for each of the articles that you summarized earlier. Each paragraph will state the findings of each article in about three or four sentences. It may also have a brief critique of each article. *Please remember that every fact you state must have an in-text APA or BPS style citation or reference.* You should have numerous references in this section, including **at least one** in each paragraph.

When complete, you should have roughly eight to ten paragraphs in this section, each one with an article that either supports your hypothesis or contradicts it. The majority of the articles that you summarize should support your hypothesis, and those should come first. The few remaining articles that contradict your hypothesis should come last. Be sure to use transitional sentences to introduce which articles support your hypothesis, and then another transitional sentence when you introduce articles that contradict it. Once you have finished these sections, you are ready to state your hypothesis(es).

**Stating Your Hypotheses**

When you state your hypothesis, or hypotheses, you do not need a new heading and sometimes you do not even need a new paragraph. This depends, however, on how long your hypotheses are and how many claims you are making. Be sure that your hypotheses are *directional*: they must state if the IV *increases* or *decreases* the DV. Try to avoid making claims like "the IV will *influence* or *affect* or *change* the DV," as those are non-directional and not precise enough to be true hypotheses. Also, be sure to state your hypotheses in the past tense and use third person (avoid terms like "I, we, us," etc.). Here are some possible hypothesis statements:

> *The present study hypothesized that participants who received ten hours of Cognitive Behavioral Therapy over a ten-week period would experience less severe symptoms of depression than participants who did not receive any Cognitive Behavioral Therapy.*

A hypothesis can also be more complex:

> *The present study hypothesized that men over the age of 50 would experience less depression after receiving ten weeks of Cognitive Behavioral Therapy, compared to men of that same age range who do not receive any Cognitive Behavioral Therapy. It was also hypothesized that women of all ages would experience less depression after ten weeks of Cognitive Behavioral Therapy, compared to women who did not receive the same therapy treatment.*

Once you have completed your hypothesis statement(s), you have finished your literature review and are ready to move on to the methods section, which we will talk about in the next chapter.

# 10  Writing a Methods Section

Now that you have completed your introduction and literature review, it's time to move on to the *Methods* section. The methods section has a very different feel than the introduction and literature review. **The purpose of the methods section is to show your readers exactly how you conducted your study, and thus is extremely detailed and strictly factual.** Since you are writing in APA, remember to always write in third person and only in past tense. First person terms like *I, we, us,* and *our group* are not used because it is less scientific and too intimate of a way to report information. Third person, past tense phrases used in research papers may

DOI: 10.4324/9781003099369-10

sound, for example, like: *the researchers examined, the team studied,* and *the students evaluated.*

**This portion of your paper is all about details. You must write with enough detail so that another researcher can replicate or repeat your study exactly as you did it.** In order for this to be possible, it is important for you and your fellow researchers to describe everything, including the physical environment (like location, time of day, and objects within the environment) and all measurement tools (such as depression tests, memory tests, etc.). Let me elaborate on this concept in a bit more detail … Let's say that you conduct your experiment in a study room in your college library. Is it acceptable to state in your methods section that *the present experiment was conducted in a study room within the college library*? That unfortunately does not include enough detail to allow proper replication of the study. What your description should say is something along the lines of, *the present study was conducted in a 4 ft. by 6 ft. white colored room located in the college library containing one table, two desk chairs, and an analog clock.* Although it may seem like that last sentence was suffocating with unnecessary details, they are in fact extremely necessary. As a psychology student you will learn, if you haven't already, that the human mind is highly complex and its functioning can be swayed by even the tiniest of details, such as an analog clock being located on the east wall of a study room vs. a room with no clock at all. And those types of differences can hold the power to significantly alter a study's results if they are not properly taken into account and controlled.

On a similar note, can you as a researcher state, *the participants' depression levels were measured using a depression test*? Again, the answer is no. You need to provide much more information than that, as there are many different depression scales out there that could be used. Instead, you could say: ***the Beck Depression Inventory (BDI) was used to measure participants' depression levels.*** You would also need to reference the research article where you found the BDI scale and include reliability and validity information about the test, including information on how often it has been used in the past by other researchers. This will show your readers that the BDI is a commonly used test that is reliable and valid, both of which are necessary requirements for any measure.

There are many reasons why you need to include so much detail. One reason is that the test you use, or the room that you use, can affect the results of your study. For example, if you do a study on anxiety and you use a bright red room instead of a plain white one, the color difference has the potential to affect the participants' mood and may directly result in higher-than-normal anxiety levels. Another reason why it is important to use so many details in your methods section is due to what is known as the *replication crisis*.

**The replication crisis is a common issue that can be found in scientific communities across the globe.** *Replication crisis* **is a term that has been used to describe the phenomenon of published, highly accepted research studies that, when they are replicated, are deemed obsolete due to error. There have been many published**

**research studies in psychology that, when another researcher tries to duplicate those studies, the new researcher gets very different results than the original researcher. Some of these flawed studies are famous enough to have once been found in introductory psychology textbooks that were used in thousands of classrooms across the world.** This is a huge problem in research that is still prevalent within the scientific community, and unfortunately nobody is completely sure how to deal with it. One way of diminishing this issue is by researchers reporting their methods of performing a study with an abundance of accurate and detailed information.

With those issues in mind, it is now time to look at how to write an effective and accurate methods section. An APA-style methods section has three key subsections: *participants*, *apparatus and materials*, and *procedures*. When you start writing this part of your paper and create each of the three subsections, be sure to use the correct level and formatting for the APA headings. For example, when you create a methods section, you start with a level-1 heading that looks like this:

## Methods

Please note that the word *Methods* is centered and in bold. Next, you will have a level 2 heading right underneath the word *Methods* that is also bold but flush left rather than centered. Your first level 2 heading will be the word *Participants* (see the following).

### Participants

There are several things to know about the *Participants* subsection. The first is that you always use the word "Participants" and not "Subjects," as it is an old term that is no longer used to describe experiments involving humans. The term "Subjects" can, however, still be used to describe animal participants in a study. The *Participants* section includes several key details, including how many people were in the study, where they were recruited from, and their basic demographics (only those who are relevant to your study). So, if age, race, or gender were variables analyzed in your study, be sure to include the percentages of your population that fall into each group. Here is an example:

---

**Participants**

*The present study included 100 participants recruited from a medium-sized community college in Southern California. The age range was 18–36 with a mean age of 20. The sample from this study was 48% male and 52% female, 48% of which were White, 38% Latinx, and 14% Asian American.*

---

This subsection might be as short as what has been shown; however, if there are additional relevant variables that will be examined in your study, you should include them here. For example, if all participants were recruited from the school's football team, or half of the sample was recruited from the LGBTQ+ community, or if a significant number of your participants were members of a particular socioeconomic status (SES), those variables should also be included.

Anything that illustrates the uniqueness of your population should be reported at this point in your research paper. One thing to note: when you report numbers or percentages always use the number, such as "12" rather than the word "twelve," unless the very first word of a sentence is a number. For example, *One hundred students participated in the present study with an age range of 18–36 years.* Notice that "one hundred" is spelled out, while "18–36" was given in numbers. It is important to write this way so that numbers do not accidentally look like a data value as they would if they were placed next to a period symbol.

The next subsection is titled *Apparatus and Materials*, or sometimes just *Materials*. In this section, it is your job to thoroughly describe all of the equipment, surveys, tests, and any additional materials used in your study. Use a level-2 header to begin this section, as shown later.

## Materials

Note that the word *Materials* is in bold and left flush on the page. Right underneath the word *Materials*, you will use a level-3 header for the first item, or apparatus, used in your study. Just for an example's sake, let's say that you used a demographics survey in your study first. The level-3 heading will look like this:

### Demographics Survey

Note that *Demographics Survey* is in bold, italics, and flush left. In this paragraph you should include a detailed overview of the item. For example, you could write:

---

*Demographics Survey*

A demographics survey was used to collect general information about the study's participants. Questions on this survey included asking participants for their age, gender, ethnicity, and annual income.

---

Keep in mind that another researcher should be able to replicate your study using the exact same questions you used. Therefore, it may be advantageous for you to provide a copy of the survey that you used in your Appendix at the end of your paper and reference it here. If there is not enough detail in your report to replicate the survey, or other measurement tools, researchers won't be able to run your study and repeat your results. Once you have completed the description of the first item, you move to the next one that you used. Be sure to start a new paragraph and use another level-3 heading for each individual item, as you see later for *PowerPoint Slides*. Once you name the item, you describe it just as you did before, with as much details as possible.

---

*PowerPoint Slides*

Participants in this study were shown a total of five PowerPoint slide decks. Each slide contained one of five words, in the following order: dog, cat, bird, wolf, sheep. All slides had a blue background and the letters for each word were in white, using a Times New Roman 36-point font. Participants sat approximately one foot away from the computer when they viewed the slides.

---

Once you have included information on every piece of equipment used (including computers, food, software, study rooms, surveys, tests, sound machines, EKGs, etc.), you have finished the *Materials* subsection. It is then time to move on to the final methods subsection, titled *Procedures*.

### Procedures

For the *Procedures* heading, you use a level-2 heading, as seen earlier. You may find the procedures subsection to be the most enjoyable part of the methods section to write because it is fairly straightforward. You will most likely find the *Procedures* subsection a lot easier to write if you have already run at least one participant through your entire experiment. You can run this participant through a pilot study, a manipulation check, or even the official experiment. Either way, it will give you all of the information necessary to write the procedures properly. If you are not familiar with pilot studies or manipulation checks, you may want to review these topics in your class textbook (if available) or ask your professor for more information.

Not every student or group will have the opportunity to run a pilot study or manipulation check. However, if you or your group can run just one participant through the entire study, it will help smooth out the procedures section. There are other benefits too, first being that when you initially begin running your experiment, you will inevitably encounter some problems. It's best to face and fix these problems before you recruit large groups of participants. It is highly recommended that you ask one or two fellow students from your research methods class, preferably someone that doesn't know much about your study, and run them through your entire experiment. That way you will be able to see what works—or what doesn't—and you can also get honest feedback from your peers as to what they liked or didn't like about your study. This type of feedback can be rare in studies that do not include a pilot because strangers are much less likely to feel comfortable critiquing your work. Once you have run these one or two practice participants and fine-tuned your study's procedures, then you are ready to run real participants and report how you did this in your *Procedures* section.

Now, the purpose of this portion of your paper is to write a detailed, step-by-step narration of everything that your participants went through in your experiment. This includes everything that the researchers said and did with the participants, from the moment the researcher first met them to when the participant left the study. Again, it is very important not to leave out any details since other researchers who want to replicate your study will look for critical information from your procedures section.

Here are a couple additional tips for writing your procedures section. First, be sure to describe how participants were assigned to conditions. Did you use random assignment? If so, how did you carry this out? Second, be sure to clearly identify all of your independent, dependent, and extraneous variables. Remember that although you are familiar with your study, your readers are not, and what might seem very clear to you may not be clear to them.

After you have written your procedures section, you may want to have a classmate who is not familiar with your study read it and tell you if they could replicate your study based on what they just read. Chances are you will need to include more details after your classmate reads this part of your paper. Ask them if they can envision running the entire experiment step by step. If they can do it from what you have written, you have provided a thorough procedures section.

Finally, be sure to include any instructions that were given to participants using the exact words the researchers communicated to the participants. It is key that every participant gets the exact same instructions, as this can affect the results. Remember our credo: *there is no such thing as too many details, as long as you stay focused.* Once you have finished authoring your study's procedures, you have completed the *Methods* section and will then move on to reporting your study's results, which Lindsay will walk you through next in Chapter 11.

# 11 Writing a Results Section and Reporting Statistics

Following the methods section comes perhaps one of the driest parts of your experimental paper: the *Results* section. This portion of a research paper is most students' least favorite to write (from what I found from my personal peers), as it is very statistic-language heavy and does not allow for any interpretation. It includes raw numbers and values that tell readers what was found *statistically* and whether the study's hypotheses were supported or not. Now, the results section can only be written after you have run your experiment, gathered data, and performed statistical tests to evaluate your hypotheses. **In this chapter, we will start by talking about the different statistical tests that you can choose from to analyze your data, and when to use them. Then we will talk more about what goes into a results section and how to report your statistical results properly in APA format. Lastly, we will discuss how to format results tables and create visually dynamic (and APA compliant) figures.**

DOI: 10.4324/9781003099369-11

Before you can begin writing your results section, you will need to run some statistical tests on your raw data. Hopefully your professor has already discussed the different types of statistical tests at least a little bit, as we will only go over them briefly here. What follows is some information on *chi-square, correlation, t-test, regression,* and *ANOVA* (including *one-way, factorial, repeated measures,* and *mixed* designs) that may be helpful for you in deciding which test(s) need to be used to analyze your data.

## Chi-Square

There are two types of chi-square tests that can be used. The first is a *goodness of fit* test, in which your observed data values are compared to their expected values in order to determine if your data is representative of the target population. The second chi-square test you can use is a *test of independence.* This type of chi-square will determine any differences among groups in your data (e.g. sex—male vs. female). It can only be used when each of your data's categories are completely independent of one another, meaning that there is no cross-over between your groups. Due to the nature of these tests, you will most likely use the chi-square test of independence much more often than the goodness of fit test when having to do it by hand. The good news about using statistical software such as SPSS to run the *Pearson Chi-Square* is that it automatically runs both of these for you. Look at the following for a list of values you will need to be knowledgeable of and able to interpret when running a chi-square test.

> **Chi-Square (X²) Statistic**—The value that will result from your $X^2$ test. This value is compared to the values in a chi-square critical value table to determine, based on your degrees of freedom, if it is significant.
> **Degrees of Freedom (df)**—A number that represents how much variance is allowed—based on the number of values—in a statistical analysis.
> **Sample Size (N)**—The number of participants included in a statistical analysis.
> **P-Value (p)**—A value that is compared to a set significance level (usually $p = .05$) to determine if the results of a statistical test are significant. If $p < .05$, then it is considered significant. However, if $p > .05$, then it is not significant.

## Test of Independence

Hypotheses

- $H_O$: (*variable A*) and (*variable B*) are independent.
- $H_A$: (*variable A*) and (*variable B*) are not independent.

Degrees of Freedom

- $df = (k - 1)$
- $k$ is the number of *categories*

Results Statement

- The relationship between (*variable A*) and (*variable B*) is/is not statistically significant, $X^2(df, N) = $ *chi-square value*, $p = $ *p-value*.

**Example:** *You are performing a study on teenagers (ages 13 to 17) to determine if daily caloric intake significantly differs between males and females.*

Hypotheses

- $H_O$: *Biological sex* and *daily caloric intake* are independent.
- $H_A$: *Biological sex* and *daily caloric intake* are not independent.

$X^2$ Statistic

- $X^2 = 5.32$

Degrees of Freedom

- $df = (k - 1)$
  $df = (2 - 1)$
  $df = 1$

P-Value

- $p = .027$

Results Statement

- The relationship between *gender* and *daily caloric intake* in teenagers is statistically significant, $X^2(1, 50) = 5.32, p = .03$.

*Correlation*

A *correlation* is a statistical test that is used to identify directional associations among variables. Although I am almost positive you have been told this at least once or twice by your professor before reading it here … **correlation does not imply causation.** A correlational relationship can only claim that there is a positive, negative, or non-existing association between two or more variables. It cannot, however, back up the claim that one variable has *caused* another to change or trend in a particular way. Similar to the chi-square test of independence, you will need to have a few pieces of information, this time including a new statistic, "*r*."

*Correlation Coefficient (r)*—A coefficient of either positive or negative value given from a statistical test for correlation that indicates the strength and direction of an association between variables.

A correlation's strength is given by how close the *r* value is to *0* or *+/−1*. An *r* value closer to *+/−1* is considered stronger than one closer to *0*. A positive *r* value indicates that when one variable increases, so does the other. A negative *r* value, however, indicates an inverse relationship in which one variable increases while the other decreases.

***Effect Size***—A classification of the strength of a correlation based on a scale derived from the value of the correlation coefficient. Various scales exist based on different statistical research findings, and depending on which one your professor uses, the cut-off values may change. But, as I used in my advanced statistical course, and according to the work of Cohen (1988, 1992), here are some accurate effect size values that can be used to determine effect size:

- $r = 0.1$ small
- $r = 0.3$ medium
- $r = 0.5$ strong

### Hypotheses

- $H_O$: The correlation coefficient of (*variable A*) and (*variable B*) is equal to zero.
- $H_A$: The correlation coefficient of (*variable A*) and (*variable B*) is not equal to zero.

### Degrees of Freedom

- $df = N - 2$

### Results Statement

The correlation coefficient There was a *(effect size) (direction)* correlation between (*variable A*) and (*variable B*), $r$ *(df)* = *r statistic*, $p = $ *p-value*.

**Example:** *You and some fellow researchers are conducting a study on the relationship between ice cream sales and drowning instances in the summertime.*

### Hypotheses

- $H_O$: The correlation coefficient of *ice cream sales* and *drowning instances* is equal to zero.
- $H_A$: The correlation coefficient of *ice cream sales* and *drowning instances* is not equal to zero.

### Correlation Coefficient

- $r = .89$

Degrees of Freedom

- $df = N - 2$
  $df = 100 - 2$
  $df = 98$

P-Value

- $p = .00001$

Results Statement

- There was a strong positive correlation between *ice cream sales* and *drowning instances*, $r(98) = .89$, $p < .001$.

## T-Test

The purpose of a t-test is to determine the differences between mean values within a data set. Depending on what your data looks like, you will have to perform one of three different types: (1) one-sample, (2) independent sample, or (3) paired sample. The one-sample t-test is used when you are interested in comparing the mean of one sample within your data to one absolute value (usually an already established mean value found outside of your data). The independent samples t-test would be used instead if you wanted to compare the means of two completely independent groups within your data. And a paired sample t-test is used to compare the means of one group within your data at two different time points. An example of an independent samples t-test is provided next.

### Independent Samples T-Test

Hypotheses

- $H_O$: The means of (*group A*) and (*group B*) are equal.
- $H_A$: The means of (*group A*) and (*group B*) are not equal.

Degrees of Freedom

- $df = N - 2$

Results Statement

- There was/was not a statistically significant difference in the mean (*Dependent Variable*) between (*group 1*) and (*group 2*), $t(df) = t\text{-value}$, $p = p\text{-value}$.

**Example:** *You are running a study to determine if the mean IQ value for high school students differs between lower-classmen (9th and 10th grade) and upper-classmen (11th and 12th grade).*

Hypotheses

- $H_O$: The mean IQ values of *lower-classmen* and *upper-classmen* are equal.
- $H_A$: The mean IQ values of *lower-classmen* and *upper-classmen* are not equal.

T-Value

- $t = 1.285$

Degrees of Freedom

- $df = N - 2$
  $df = 2000 - 2$
  $df = 1998$

P-Value

- $p = .337$

Results Statement

- There was not a statistically significant difference in the mean IQ between high school *lower-classmen* and *upper-classmen*, $t(1998) = 1.29, p = .33$.

## *ANOVA*

ANOVA, or analysis of variance, tests are similar to the t-test in that they indicate statistically significant differences between mean values. Where ANOVA differs is in its ability to compare means for more than two variables at one time. Its results will indicate if there is overall significance between your variables, including what are called *interaction effects* occurring between the tested groups. What an ANOVA test alone fails to tell you is exactly where the significance is coming from among your tested variables. To find that out, you would have to run a post hoc test to follow up your original findings, which we will talk about later on in this chapter.

There are a few different types of ANOVA tests, but the main three you will most likely encounter in your class are one-way, two-way, and repeated measures. A *one-way ANOVA* is run on data that only has two variables, one dependent and one independent. In a one-way analysis, the independent variable must have two or more independent groups which can be compared to one another. For example, a study interested in understanding the effects of different forms of exercise on feelings of self-worth could run a one-way ANOVA on self-worth and their three types of exercise: walking, swimming, and weight-lifting. In this example, feelings of self-worth acts as the dependent variable while exercise is the independent variable. Exercise was broken up into three subcategories or groups, and these become the levels within the one-way analysis whose mean values are compared to one another.

A *two-way ANOVA* is similar in that it still compares mean values between variables but includes two independent variables instead of one. This analysis additionally evaluates what is known as an *interaction*, which indicates if the effects of the first independent variable influence the effects of the second independent variable on the dependent variable, and vice versa. For example, let's say you are running a study to see if sugar intake and/or amount of nightly sleep have any effects on concentration levels in college students while in a classroom setting. Your sugar intake variable consists of two groups (high sugar and low sugar) while your sleep variable consists of three groups (< 8 hours, 8 hours, > 8 hours). A two-way ANOVA would indicate main effects (whether or not either of the two variables have an effect on concentration levels) as well as any possible interaction effects (e.g. do the effects of sugar intake influence how nightly sleep effects concentration?). A one- or two-way ANOVA can become a *repeated measures ANOVA (rmANOVA)* when only one group of participants is used for all of the variable conditions, just at different points in time. An *rmANOVA* can only be used as long as the effects of the earlier conditions do not carry over and affect the later conditions.

The ANOVA test's abilities do, however, have a limit: it only tells you if there is a significant overall effect between your variables. It cannot, on its own, indicate which variables are responsible for the in/significant findings. The same holds true for interactions: if there was an interaction found between your two independent variables, the two-way ANOVA would not be able to indicate the mechanisms behind that interaction. In other words, if we went back to the sugar and sleep example, you would know that there was an interaction occurring between sugar intake, amount of sleep, and concentration levels, but you would not have any indication as to which of those variables were driving the interaction. In order to evaluate this, a follow-up post hoc test and some simple effects testing would have to be used. Although you may run into post hoc testing in introductory research methods, you will most likely not see simple effects testing until you get to higher level statistics courses.

There are many types of post hoc tests used in statistics today, but only a few are usually taught in undergraduate research methods: *Fisher's LSD, Tukey HSD, Scheffe,* and *Bonferroni. Fisher's LSD* is the most lenient of these tests and therefore is often avoided unless an adjusted alpha level is calculated and used (again, something you will probably not run into until advanced statistics). The *Bonferroni* test is often used instead; however, many professors from higher statistics courses have recently criticized it as too conservative. *Scheffe's* test is also known to be strict, but it can be very useful when you have groups of unequal sizes. Lastly, the *Tukey HSD* test sort of falls in the middle with regards to stringency and is often used along with the *Bonferroni* test.

Hypotheses—Main Effects

- $H_O$: There are no differences in (*DV*) based on (*IV*).
- $H_A$: There are differences in (*DV*) based on (*IV*).

*★Note*: If you are running a factorial ANOVA, you will have several sets of hypotheses statements: one for each independent variable that is included in the analysis.

Hypotheses—Interaction

- $H_O$: There are no differences in (*DV*) based on the interaction of (*IV$_1$*) and (*IV$_2$*).
- $H_A$: There are differences in (*DV*) based on the interaction of (*IV$_1$*) and (*IV$_2$*).

Degrees of Freedom

- $df = N - k$
- $k$ is the number of samples

Results Statements

- Main effects:
  There was/was not a statistically significant effect of (*IV*) on *(DV)*, $F(df_1, df_2)$ = F-value, $p$ = ___, $\eta^2$ = ___.
- Interaction:
  There was/was not a statistically significant interaction between (*IV$_1$*) and (*IV$_2$*) on (*DV*).

### Figures—Tables and Graphs

After analyzing your data from the statistical testing, you may then want to make some visual aids to help your readers better understand the results. The types of visual aids most commonly used in research articles are tables and graphs. When creating tables and graphs, it is important to be sure to follow the formatting guidelines from APA (or BPS if that is what your professor prefers), as it will outline how the figure should look. What is included in

Table 1.1 Correlations Between Instances of Adultery and Age, Self-Esteem, Relationship Satisfaction, and Locus of Control Measures.

| Variable | x̄ | SD | N | r | Sig. 2-tailed |
|---|---|---|---|---|---|
| Age | 22.48 | 7.46 | 196 | −.149 | .034★ |
| Self-Esteem | 3.27 | .41 | 198 | −.202 | .003★ |
| LOC Internality | 4.86 | .64 | 198 | −.178 | .018★ |
| LOC Powerful Others | 2.99 | .77 | 198 | .191 | .010★ |
| LOC Chance | 2.85 | .68 | 198 | .222 | .002★ |
| Relationship Satisfaction | 7.71 | 1.34 | 198 | .100 | .126 |
| Instances of Adultery | 3.55 | 1.05 | 198 | | |

★$p < .05$

your table or graph will be entirely contingent upon the nature of your study; however, a lot of studies will include data values that display the statistical significance of each variable, including means, standard deviations, and p-values. Other values that are often included in tables in particular is the N (sample size) and the statistical coefficient, whether it is a *t*, *r*, or *F* value.

The following is an example of a table portraying data from a hypothetical study evaluating any associations between the overall instances of adultery confessed by married couples and other variables, such as age, self-esteem, locus of control, and relationship satisfaction. The data provided in Table 1.1 are hypothetical only and do not represent results from an actual study.

Now, here is an example of an entire results section as well as some graphs that I produced back in my undergraduate studies as a biopsychology student at Cal State Fullerton. While in that class, my fellow students and I participated in a study run by our professor and then were asked to analyze our raw data and provide results. In the study, each of our blood glucose levels were measured at four different time points after ingesting a food item containing either high-fructose corn syrup or natural sugar. The figures given next were made to display any relationships found between time, the type of food eaten, and the participants' biological sex.

## Results

A mixed-design ANOVA was conducted using the IBM SPSS Statistics software to determine whether there were statistically significant differences in blood glucose levels based on the main and interaction effects of gender, food condition, and time. All assumptions were assumed met based on preliminary data analysis. The results indicated blood glucose levels to be the highest on average at T1

(148.18 ± 16.27), which occurred 20 minutes following food consumption (see Figure 11.1 for overall average blood glucose levels). The main effect of time resulted in a statistically significant difference in blood glucose levels, $F(3) = 9.56$, $p < .001$, with T1 showing significant mean differences between T0 ($p < .001$), T2 ($p = .008$), and T3 ($p < .001$). Individuals assigned to the No HFCS food condition had the highest average blood glucose levels (153.20 ± 17.08) compared to the HFCS group (144 ± 15.80) indicated at T1 (see Figure 11.2 for average blood glucose levels based on food condition). The main effect for food condition resulted in a statistically non-significant difference in blood glucose levels, $F(1, 8) = .52$, $p = .49$. Average blood glucose levels were recorded highest for females at T1 (149.40 ± 16.61), as indicated in Figure 11.3. The main effect of gender resulted in a statistically non-significant difference in blood glucose levels, $F(1, 8) = 2.55$, $p = .14$. The interaction effect between food condition and time resulted in a non-significant difference in blood glucose levels, $F(3, 10) = 1.96$, $p = .14$. Although an interaction effect appeared to be possible between food condition and gender (as indicated in Figures 11.1, 11.2, 11.3 respectively), statistics were unable to be assessed due to the absence of male cases in the HFCS food condition.

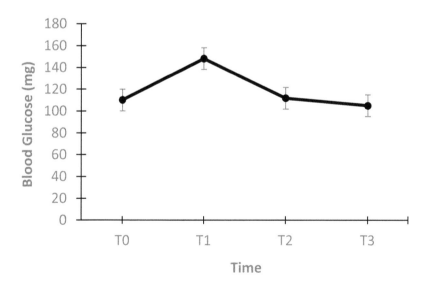

*Figure 11.1* Overall mean blood glucose levels over the four time measurement points. Significant differences were found between the effects of time on blood glucose levels. Standard errors of the means are represented in the figure by the error bars attached to each time point.

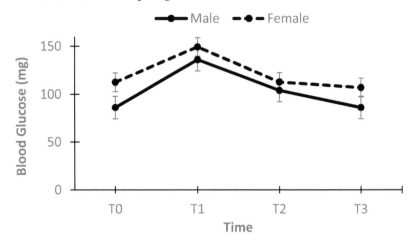

*Figure 11.2* Mean blood glucose levels for both males and females at each measurement time point. No differences in blood glucose levels were found based on the effects of gender. Standard errors of the means are represented in the figure by the error bars attached to each time point.

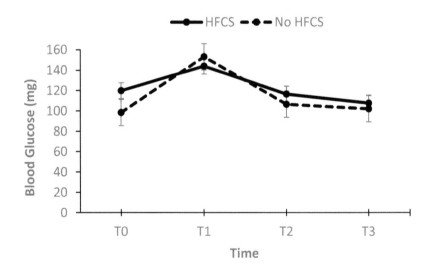

*Figure 11.3* Mean blood glucose levels for the HFCS group and the no HFCS group, at all four measurement time points. No blood glucose level differences were found based on the effects of food condition group membership. Standard errors are represented in the figure by the error bars attached to each time point.

# References

Cohen, J. (1988). *Statistical power analysis for the behavioral sciences* (2nd ed.). Hillside, NJ: Lawrence Erlbaum.

Cohen, J. (1992). A power primer. *Psychological Bulletin, 112,* 155–159. doi: 10.1037/0033-2909.112.1.155

# 12 Writing a Discussion Section

The discussion section immediately follows your results section. It will include similar ideas as your results section, but thankfully it is a lot more fun to write due to its more creative and fluid nature. The discussion section still has some rules you will have to follow, but there are far less than you ran across in any other section of your paper. We both agree that the discussion is the most enjoyable section to write in a paper, because you not only get to tell the world about your results but also to *interpret* them and explain why they are important. It is also more creative than the other sections, given that you can be more flexible with the content. Before starting your own discussion section, remember to format the title correctly. It should look like this, centered and boldface:

### Discussion

So, what should be found in a discussion section? **Well, the first thing that should be included is a restatement of your findings.** Most individuals

DOI: 10.4324/9781003099369-12

usually start their discussion by first restating their hypotheses and then noting whether or not those hypotheses were supported by the study. **You will not want to use the same statistical language to explain your findings here as you did in your results section, because you have already done so.** In the discussion, you should **focus on words and descriptions** rather than numbers and values.

The discussion section is sometimes described as the opposite of a literature review. This can be a beneficial way to look at it when writing your own discussion. In the literature review, you begin with very general ideas and claims but then end up with a narrow and focused hypothesis. In the discussion section, on the other hand, you start off with the narrow hypothesis, describing whether or not it was supported, and then you more broadly explain the findings of your study. So, in a way, the structure and flow of each section are somewhat opposites.

Here is an example for how to start off this section of your paper:

---

### Discussion

The present study examined the influence of exercise on energy levels in teenaged boys. It was hypothesized that a 30-minute exercise regimen would enhance the energy level of all participants. Results demonstrated that male participants between the ages of 13 to 16 years who completed the 30-minute workout had 10% more energy than those in the same age bracket who did not complete the workout. However, the boys between the ages of 16 to 18 years who completed the 30-minute workout showed no improvement in energy level when compared to those that did not complete the workout. Thus, the hypothesis was only partially confirmed, as only younger teenage boys tended to benefit from the exercise regimen.

---

When writing in APA format, you want to keep your writing direct and to-the-point. It is not necessary or recommended to use a lot of extra or "fluffy" language in an experimental paper. Say what you need to say, and then move on. Now that you have stated the findings of your paper, you can explain what they mean in more detail.

The next topic you may want to talk about in your discussion section is: *how did the results of your study relate to the research you discussed in the Literature Review?* If your current results replicated the results of some of the previous studies cited, discuss the similarities between your results and those previous studies. If your results were different from previous studies, explain why you think that they did not match up with the studies introduced in the literature review. You can do this easily by answering one question:

*what was different about your study compared to the ones you cited in the Literature Review?*

Be sure to properly cite information from past studies you mention from your literature review **again** when you mention it for the second time in your discussion section. For example:

> *The results of the present study were very similar to the study conducted by Jones (2018) discussed earlier. Both studies noted that younger teenage boys benefited more from the short exercise workout compared to older teenage boys. This finding might have occurred because the boys selected for the current study used the exact same workout as the boys in the Jones (2018) study.*

If your study had different findings than the research discussed in the literature review, be sure to offer what you believe the reason to be for that finding. Try not to use grandiose explanations, but rather one or two simple explanations for your findings. For example:

> *The current study demonstrated somewhat different results than the Smith (2019) study. The current study showed a benefit for the younger teenagers that completed the exercise workout, whereas the Smith (2019) study did not show that benefit. One possible explanation would be that the populations were quite different in each study. The current study used high school students from a large urban high school, and the Smith (2019) study used students from a small rural high school. It is possible that differences in diet, culture, or physical activity outside of school created those differences.*

**Once you have thoroughly stated your findings and how they were similar and/or different than the previous literature, you might want to note any unique findings of your study that have not already been noted in the discussion section.** For example, perhaps the exercise regimen you implemented caused some negative impacts on your teens. Maybe those that did not participate in the exercise regimen had negative results other than a reduction in energy. On the other hand, it is entirely possible that you will not have any unique findings to report at this point.

**After stating the differences or uniqueness of your study, you then want to move on to what can be considered the "heart" of your discussion: what the results *actually mean* for the rest of the world.** In other words, how do your results generalize and help people outside of your study? If the purpose of research is to make people's lives better, this is your opportunity to show how your study does that. How can your research be used to improve the quality of other people's lives? For instance, your study found that younger teenage boys benefited from a 30-minute workout, while the older teenage boys did not. Assuming your results are valid (later we will discuss how to state the limitations of your research), what can you now do with your findings to make other people live better and happier lives? Here is an example of how the following section might look:

---

*It was stated earlier that the younger group of teenage boys benefited from the exercise workout, while the older teenage boys did not. This new information could be helpful by changing the way physical education is taught to include only beneficial exercise. The present study showed that in large, city-based urban high schools, 30-minute exercise workouts were more beneficial for younger rather than older teenage boys. Therefore, this exercise program should only be implemented for the population that it has been shown to benefit, while new research should be conducted to find what is beneficial for the older teenage boys. Smith's (2018) research showed that a 30-minute exercise regimen was beneficial to all high school age boys; however, the participants included in that study were from a rural setting. So, the key take away from this current study is that location matters. Urban teenage boys may have different exercise needs than teenage boys who live in more rural areas.*

*Note: the passages that are included in this chapter are fabricated for the sake of example and are NOT actual results that should be used or cited as factual.

---

In my opinion, that would be the most important take away from this study because it opens the door to all sorts of future research that could be done, not only to confirm these results but also to find a new exercise program for the older boys.

**The next part of your discussion will include any limitations your research study may have suffered from.** This can include information on what you did wrong, what should have been done differently, or what you would have liked to do that was simply not possible due to your budget, available samples, etc. If this is one of the first studies you have ever done, this portion ends up being one of the easiest to write because there are usually all sorts of things that you realize after the fact could have been done differently. For example, chances are that the sample you selected for your study was not a random sample, was significantly small, or might have only included a very specific demographic compared to the rest of your state or country's general population. Topics that can be touched on while discussing the limitations of your study include the size, recruitment, or demographic of your sample, as well as a possible lack of access to equipment or ample time to run the experiment. You may also have had to deal with budgetary restrictions, equipment failures, tests or measures lacking sensitivity, flawed surveys, flaws in your design, and other problems implementing your experiment, all of which should be discussed. Here is an example of how this part of your discussion may be delivered:

*Apart from the unique findings of this research, there were also some limitations. The present study was conducted at a medium-sized high school in California, in a primarily residential neighborhood. As noted in the Participants section, the demographics are slightly skewed in this region compared to other, more urban-based high schools in California. This high school had a larger representation of Anglo and Latinx students and smaller populations of African American and Asian American students compared to other nearby high schools. Also, the sample taken from this school was a convenience sample that was limited to only 40 teenage boys in total. Another limitation of this study includes the test that was used to measure the teens' energy levels. Although this test was well standardized, it was more heavily standardized to measure energy levels in adults rather than teens or children. This lack of standardization on teens could lead to inaccuracies. Finally, due to time limitations, this study was done as a cross-sectional study rather than a longitudinal study. The current researchers were only able to track the teens' behavior over a two-week period rather than the previously mentioned research, which monitored the teens over a three-month period.*

**The final topic you will want to touch on at this point is any future research that will be conducted by the same researchers in order to further understand their topic.** Some call this the "*where to go from here*" portion of the discussion. Essentially, you will take the findings of your current research and use it to build your next, follow-up study. It might look something like this:

*Based on the unique findings of this study, the present researchers plan to engage in several future studies. The first study will focus on the differences in the efficacy of exercise programs between urban and rural teenage boys. The second study will examine the differences in the effectiveness of exercise in younger vs. older teenage boys. The current research team may also examine the effectiveness of exercise in younger and older teenage girls in both rural and urban populations.*

Once you have completed the discussion section, you are almost done with your experimental paper! You just have a few more, smaller tasks to complete before you are ready to turn in your work. We will cover those tasks in the next chapter.

# 13 Title Page, Abstract, and Checklists

## Ross

CONGRATULATIONS! You have almost reached the end of your research paper! You have now completed the literature review, methods, results, and discussion sections of your paper. There are still a few more things you will need to include in your paper before turning it in, but you have now gotten through the most difficult parts. This chapter will focus on putting some final and finishing touches on your paper, including a title page and an abstract.

When you conduct an internet search on how to create an APA title page, you might find instructions on how to complete both a *student* and a *professional* title page. As a professor, I usually tell students to use the *professional* title page. They are both actually quite similar; however, the professional

DOI: 10.4324/9781003099369-13

one is often preferred. It not only looks better but is also what your professor will be used to seeing (and the one they will most likely just require you to use). It only takes a few minutes to create a professional title page, whereas a *student* title page is a bit more time consuming.

The first thing you will need to do when creating a title page is to look up on your word processor how to create a running head as well as page numbers (only if you haven't done this before). The running head and page numbers both start on the title page and are mandatory on every following page in your document. The running head is a very brief version of your title, roughly about three to five words, that is written in all capital lettering. It will be placed in the upper left-hand corner of each page. To create the running head, look up the terms *heading* or *header and footer* in your word processor's *Help* menu. This will help you create a correctly formatted running head. Using the same help menu, you can also look up *page numbers.* Your word processer will give you several options for where to place the page numbers, and this is where you will choose to place them in the upper right-hand corner of each page. Once you enter it onto the first page, it will automatically show up on all the others.

Now, the tricky thing with the running head is that in APA formatting the first page looks slightly different than all the rest. On your title page, the running head has to include the words *"Running head"* before your abbreviated title:

| |
|---|
| Running head: INSERT ABBREVIATED TITLE HERE          1 |

On all following pages, your running head will only include the same abbreviated title as your first running head:

| |
|---|
| INSERT ABBREVIATED TITLE HERE                                          2 |

If you are using Microsoft Word as your word processor, you can do this by double-clicking your current header and then checking the box *"Different First Page"* on the menu that pops up at the top. You may have to re-type one or both of your titles one more time to get the correct format, but hopefully that will do the trick. If not, try typing *header* into the *Help* menu and see if the option for a different first page pops up that way.

Lindsay and I both understand that having to go through all of this work to get a proper running head and page numbers inserted into your paper may seem like a waste of time, but it served an important purpose back in the day. The initial purpose of the running head goes back to the days when people would mail in printed copies of their manuscripts. In the event that someone unfortunately dropped an un-stapled manuscript, the running head would help them identify all of the pages that belong together in a document. The page numbering would then help to keep the manuscript in its correct order. Although most—if not all—manuscripts are now shared electronically, the running head has remained in the APA Publication Manual as a formatting requirement.

Once you have inserted a running head and page numbers, the rest will hopefully be quite easy. The next step is to add in the full title of your paper, followed by the names of all authors (first name, middle initial, and last name) and each of the authors' affiliations or college(s) where they attend or work. Note that for a student paper, you will probably only be entering only your own name rather than the names of everyone in your group, assuming that your professor requires you to write your own paper. If your paper was collectively written by your entire group, then you would want to include the names of everyone on the title page. If you are unsure how to record authorship of your paper, my advice is to ask your professor what he/she prefers. In my research methods class, each experiment is carried out in groups, but every student writes their own separate paper. As a result, I ask that students only record their own name on the title page.

When it comes to entering the title of your paper as well as your name and affiliation, there are a few simple rules to follow. The title of your paper should be placed approximately three to four rows down from the top of the title page, centered and boldface, and you should capitalize the major words of the title. The author name(s) will come next, on the line directly underneath the title. If you need to include two authors, use the word "and" between the two names. If there are three or more authors, you would put a comma after each name and the word "and" before the final author's name.

For the author's affiliation, move to the next line and list the name of your department followed by a comma, and then the name of your college or university. The final part of the title page is known as the Author's Note; however, your professor will likely not require you to include this in your title page. Here is an example of what a professional APA title page might look like:

---

**The Effects of Cognitive Behavioral Therapy on Major Depression:**

**A clinical study**



Ross A. Seligman

Department of Psychology, Citrus College

Lindsay Mitchell

Department of Psychology, California State University, Fullerton

---

Now that you have completed your APA title page, it is finally time to learn how to write an abstract. An abstract is essentially a summary of your entire paper written in no more than 250 words. As a general rule, each section of your paper—the introduction, methods, results, and discussion—should only take up one to two sentences of your abstract. It is no accident that we talk about the abstract last, as the abstract *should* be written after the entire paper has already been completed. If you think about it, a summary in any other instance can only be created for a piece of writing that has already been written. Although it is technically possible to write your abstract first, it will be much easier to do so after you have already written the rest of your paper.

Let's start with some basic formatting rules for the abstract. Your abstract should always be placed on its own page, immediately following your title page. You should already have a running head and page number on this page, but as was mentioned earlier, you will have to modify the running head on this page (and all following ones if it is not done automatically) to no longer include the words "*Running head.*" As always, make sure that you have one-inch margins and are using double spacing, third person, and past tense. Start off your first line with the word *Abstract.* Make sure it is capitalized, boldface, and centered on the top of the page like so:

---

INSERT ABBREVIATED TITLE HERE                                            1
**Abstract**

---

You will want to start the text of your abstract on the next line down. **Do not skip a line, do not indent the first sentence,** and be sure to use a standard font such as Times New Roman in 12-point font. An abstract is recommended to be a minimum of 150 words but cannot exceed 250 words, so you will have to choose carefully what to include. Once you have completed your paragraph, drop down to the next line and indent that line 0.5 inches. After the indent, type in: "*Keywords:*" and include a few key terms that would help a reader find your article in a database search engine. Write those words in lower case with commas following each word, and no period at the end. Here is an example using our exercise and energy levels example from the last chapter:

---

*Keywords: energy, energy level, exercise*

---

When you write the abstract, it is best to include a little bit about each of the following parts of your paper:

1.   The research question or hypothesis

> You might want to start the abstract with a more general introductory sentence and then attach the hypothesis after the introductory sentence. Please refer to the sample abstract attached below for an example of a more general introductory sentence and a hypothesis.

2.   A sentence or two about your experimental methodology.
3.   A sentence or two about your results.
4.   A sentence or two that sums up your discussion section.

In the abstract, you don't need any in-text references or descriptions of statistical tests. Just keep it general. It's a brief, non-technical overview of your paper designed to catch the eye of the reader to see if it has information relevant to the topic that he/she is looking for. Here is an example of what an abstract might look like (please note that the information in this abstract is hypothetical and is not based on any real studies or facts):

**Abstract**

Depression is a problem that affects millions of Americans on a daily basis and depletes the economy of billions of dollars due to missed work, medical expenses, and reduced productivity. One of the best non-medical treatments for depression is Cognitive Behavioral Therapy (CBT). CBT has previously shown to be effective in two major studies. The present study used the experimental method and examined 300 male and female adult clients diagnosed with Major Depressive Disorder. Half of all the patients received CBT whereas the other half received no therapy at all. Results of this experiment demonstrated a significant drop in depression among those in the CBT group. Results from this study can be used to help depressed adult male and female patients across the United States and Europe.

*Keywords*: Depression, cognitive behavioral therapy, treatment

Now that you have created your title page and abstract, your paper should be complete. Your final step is to go through the checklist below to make sure you have all of the correct formatting and information that is required for this paper. Once you have completed the checklist, your paper is ready to turn in. Congratulations! You are just about done with the course.

## Please Check the Box for Each Item After You Have Completed It

### General formatting issues for the entire paper

☐   1" margins on all four sides
☐   APA allows various accessible fonts. I typically use: Times New Roman 12-point font
☐   Double space all lines
☐   Text should be left justified unless otherwise indicated (such as for title page and headings)
☐   Indent the start of all paragraphs, with few exceptions (such as the abstract)
☐   Write in past tense, third person. Avoid using words such as *I, we, us, our group,* etc.

### Title Page

☐   Title page has running head (with appropriate words and capitalization) and page number
☐   Title of paper reflects what the study is about
☐   Title includes the independent and dependent variable
☐   Your name/s and affiliation/s are on the title page
☐   Title of paper is centered on the page and in bold
☐   Author/s names are centered on the page, underneath the title
☐   Author/s affiliations are centered underneath each respective name (unless all authors have the same affiliation)
☐   Author's note (if applicable)—this is usually optional for a research methods class

### Abstract

☐   Abstract states the problem that needs to be investigated by the researcher.
☐   Hypothesis is included.
☐   A brief statement about results is present.
☐   You have included an explanation of why the results are relevant and how they can be used.
☐   The abstract is between 150 and 250 words and contains at least three keywords.
☐   The abstract is on page two with a page number and running head at the top of the page.

### Introduction

☐   Starts on a new page—page 3.
☐   Includes the title of the paper as a level-1 heading (not the title "*Introduction*" for this section).

☐ The statement of the problem (the dependent variable) is present near the beginning of the paper.

☐ You have included a logical reason for why this topic is important and should be studied.

☐ Recent scholarly research from the last five years is used.

☐ Every fact taken from the research is correctly referenced in APA style.

☐ No internet research is used unless allowed by your professor.

☐ Hypothesis or hypotheses are clearly stated in past tense, third person.

☐ Hypotheses state the relationship and direction of the effect between the independent and dependent variables.

## Method

☐ Participants are thoroughly described in *Participants* subsection.

☐ Include the number of participants (using correct format for numbers), where and how they were recruited, and all relevant demographics gathered for the participants.

☐ In *Materials* subsection, you have named and described all tests, measures, and equipment.

☐ You have a paragraph for each item and a boldface header to name the tests, measures, and equipment.

☐ You included reliability and validity information where needed.

☐ You have noted where to find items in the *Appendix* section (if applicable).

☐ In the *Design* subsection, you have identified the independent and dependent variables.

☐ You describe how the experiment was designed to test the hypothesis and control any possible confounding variables.

☐ You have described the statistical tests that you are using.

☐ If you had missing or uneven data, explain why.

☐ Your *Procedures* subsection includes step-by-step and thorough detail.

## Results

☐ You started with a restatement of each hypothesis and if they were supported or not.

☐ Your hypotheses have direction (indicates if the IV increased or decreased the DV).

☐ All the relevant descriptive statistics are included, such as means, frequencies, N, n, and standard deviations.

☐ All inferential statistics are reported in APA format.

☐ It is noted if between- or within-subjects design was used (if applicable).

☐ You have noted if graphs and/or charts are in the appendix.

☐ p-values are in APA format, even if non-significant.

☐ You have not used phrases such as "*the hypothesis was proven.*" Be careful about strong or incorrect language. Instead use phrases like "*the results demonstrated.*"

## Discussion

☐ You have re-stated the basic research questions and conclusions.

☐ Results are explained in terms of their relevance to society. What do they mean? How can they be used to help people in the "real world"?

☐ You have stated what went wrong in the study. What were some limitations? Discuss flaws in the study that you could not avoid (or maybe you could have given different circumstances) such as sample size, equipment failure, biases in the sample, etc.

☐ Based on the findings of this study, you have stated what the topic or hypothesis of your next study will look like.

## References

☐ You have started on a new page for the *References* section.

☐ The word *"References"* is listed at the top of the page, capitalized and in bold.

☐ All references are in correct APA format. Be sure to have made adjustments based on what sources were used (e.g. journal articles with one or more authors, open access journals, books, websites, etc.).

☐ You correctly indented the first line of each reference.

☐ You have alphabetized your list of references by the first author's last name.

☐ If you had two or more works by the same author, they should be ordered by publication date, with the oldest entry listed first.

☐ All lines are double spaced in Times New Roman 12-point font.

☐ All references used in the paper were included in your *References* page.

## Appendices—for Graphs, Figures, Surveys, etc.

☐ All figures are formatted and captioned according to APA formatting (based on the Pub. Manual, 7th edition).

☐ All items in the appendix are also noted in the paper (e.g. *see Graph 1 in Appendix 1*).

☐ You and someone else have proofread your entire paper for spelling, grammar, and APA formatting.

# 14 How to Present Your Findings in Front of Others

**Ross**

One thing that I have learned in my years of teaching is that students fear public speaking more than any other type of assignment. I think that Jerry Seinfeld summed up this fear best when he said:

> According to most studies, people's number one fear is public speaking. Number two is death. Death is number two. Does that sound right? This means to the average person, if you go to a funeral, you're better off in the casket than doing the eulogy.
>
> (Seinfeld, 2020)

Public speaking is stressful for just about everyone, even teachers, and the only way to overcome that stress and improve your public speaking skills is

DOI: 10.4324/9781003099369-14

to practice, practice, practice. As much as you might dread it, try to take advantage of any opportunities that your professors might offer you to give a speech, especially if it's in a safe setting like a small group or classroom in front of your friends and peers. The reality is that giving an oral presentation is something that you will be doing throughout your life. Most jobs will require it and college is the best place to learn and practice this skill. Even though you may not have a job where you publicly speak every day, it's still an essential skill for many social and occupational settings as well.

When you give an oral presentation in a research methods class, there are typically two parts to it. First, you need to verbally deliver your speech, and second, you need to have some sort of visual display such as a poster or PowerPoint presentation that corresponds to your speech. This chapter will give you some practical tips for both delivering a successful speech as well as creating a good PowerPoint presentation or poster.

Before I coach you a bit on how to be a better public speaker, let's talk first about the needs of the audience. Audiences don't just want to hear a bunch of facts, even if those facts are interesting. **An audience wants to be entertained.** If you can put the audience in a good mood, they are more likely to enjoy your presentation and more likely to remember what you have said. Like so many other forms of communication, what you say is just as important as how you say it. You could be giving directions to the local library, but if you do it in a fun way, your audience will remember you, as well as what you said. Audiences also tend to have very short attention spans. Overwhelming them with facts and figures will most likely exhaust them and lead them to lose interest. So, when you give a speech with lots of information, it's important to balance out that information with stories and examples that capture an audience's attention and entertain them.

Hearing that you should learn to be an entertainer might not be what you were ready to hear about successful public speaking, but it is a very helpful skill that will give you a leg up on your peers. The truth is, most people aren't very entertaining when they give speeches. And this can often lead to a damaged self-esteem for the presenter that will only make public speaking more difficult for them. If you learn to have fun with your presenting style alongside your audience, then you will feel more successful and will hopefully learn to fear it less each time you do it. If you can bring out people's emotions, the information given in your speech also has a higher chance of being remembered. For all of these reasons, we have geared the rest of this chapter to focus a lot on the entertaining aspect of public speaking.

Now, what are the best and simplest ways to be entertaining? One very easy trick is to speak loudly. When I feel nervous, I am able to combat it by speaking more loudly, as it allows me to burn off some of that energy. It also adds some life to the presentation, rather than boring people to sleep with a low or monotone voice. Speaking in a higher volume also makes your voice sound less shaky (which is always nice) and helps get your audience's attention.

**Telling stories is also very important in a speech.** It makes your speech more interesting and allows your audience to connect more effortlessly with you. Audiences don't want to listen to 20 minutes about t-tests and correlations. They would rather hear about some personal experiences you had while you ran your experiment, especially if you have some humorous ones that can be told in a sensitive and respectful way. I remember one group in my own research methods class years ago who did a study on the topic of beauty and self-esteem. During their presentation, they told this story about how during the experiment they showed pictures of attractive women to several female participants. One female participant, upon seeing these pictures, put down the sandwich she was eating for lunch and stated that she needed to go on a diet. Although that might be painful to hear, those are the types of stories that make your presentation real.

**What about telling jokes?** You might have heard that you should start a presentation by telling a joke. For this type of presentation, I would actually strongly disagree with this approach. Jokes might sound like a good starting point, but they run the risk of come off as being insensitive due to the nature of the research we are doing. For that reason, it's best to just stick with the facts and include stories that illustrate those facts.

By far the most important tip that I can give you about delivering an effective presentation is to practice the speech as much as you can before you actually deliver it to your target audience. I would recommend that you give the entire speech in a private setting at least a handful of times, because the more times that you practice your presentation, the better you will make it sound. If you rehearse your presentation enough, you will be able to commit it to memory and when you get nervous during the presentation, you hopefully won't trip on your words as much.

**Another tip about practicing your speech is that after you rehearse it at home, you should practice it in a classroom or a setting similar to where you will be delivering the presentation.** One problem with practicing an oral presentation in your home is that you will be more relaxed and you will speak slower, so the presentation will last longer than when you are in front of the class. When you get in front of the class and your adrenaline starts to flow, you will speak a lot more quickly and the presentation will be over much sooner than you expected.

**After practicing at home and in a classroom, the final step is to practice in front of a small group of family members or friends.** That will raise the pressure just a little bit. If everything goes as expected with a small group of friends and/or family as your audience, then you are then ready to give your presentation to the entire class.

**As a final tip for giving your oral presentation, it's best to maintain as much eye contact with the audience as you can.** This can be a challenge because it means memorizing a lot of your speech as well as looking directly at your audience. Maintaining eye contact makes some people nervous. But, if you don't look to be scanning the audience and making eye contact with them, they may begin to feel disconnected with what you are saying and lose interest. Truth be told, it is not that fun to watch a speaker who just looks at their notes the entire time. One trick you might find useful if you find it too difficult to make eye contact with various audience members is to look at their foreheads instead. From even a close distance, it will seem like you are looking them in the eye, and you will be able to focus better on what you are saying instead of how uncomfortable it makes you to make eye contact with them.

**So, to review, when you are giving a speech, the most important thing is to practice your speech as much as you can in private. Once you have mastered that, you can practice in a classroom and then in front a small group. Once you are done practicing, remember to speak loudly and avoid speaking too quickly. If you can, include stories into your speech and make as much eye (or forehead) contact as you can.**

### *Visual Presentations*

Now that we have discussed some tips for speaking in front of the class, it is time to talk about visual displays, such as PowerPoints and posters. In my class, I always require a PowerPoint presentation that corresponds with the student's speech. While many professors require a PowerPoint presentation, others prefer a poster presentation. I will start by giving tips for how to give a good PowerPoint presentation. There are some clear rules that should be followed. After that, we will discuss posters.

### *PowerPoint Presentations*

There are a few common rules to follow when making PowerPoint presentations. The first rule to follow is to **put as little information on your PowerPoint slides as you can while also clearly portraying the information you need**. Putting too much information into your slides is often referred to as ***death by PowerPoint.*** When *death by PowerPoint* occurs, your audience is unable to pay attention to what you are saying due to them feeling like they are having to spend all their time reading what is on your slides. Only include the skeleton of the information you will be discussing and verbally provide the rest.

**The important thing to remember is that a PowerPoint presentation is a brief outline for your speech that should only be used as a minor guide to keep your ideas on track. Each slide should only have a few words on it; as a general rule, no more than four bullet points should be included on a single PowerPoint slide, and each bullet point should have no more than four words.** In short, less is more. If you have more than 16 words on one slide, that is already too much. You can say as much as you want in your presentation, but you don't need to put the entire speech on the slide. Otherwise, people won't be listening to what you are saying and all of our talk about being entertaining flies out the window.

**Font size is very important in a PowerPoint presentation as well.** Use a very large, clear font type such as 36-point Times New Roman. My advice is to only use font sizes of 24 point or larger, as anything smaller becomes difficult to read (especially for audience members in the back of the room). I would recommend that you bring up your PowerPoint presentation, turn on the projector, and then have someone go to the back of the room and see if your slides are readable. You should also think about your audience. If your audience is older or has poor vision, a larger font may be needed.

**Should you give your audience hand-outs of the PowerPoint presentation?** I generally do not recommend this. Hand-outs take away the audience's attention from your speech, just as heavily worded slides do. Apart from putting small amounts of information on your slides and using a large font, another rule to follow is that you should never use all capital letters on your slides. You can capitalize the start of a sentence or for individual words that need to be capitalized, but don't put an entire sentence in capitals, as it is often more difficult to read that way. Also, don't abbreviate any more than you absolutely need to because it will only confuse your audience more and defeat the purpose of effectively delivering information.

Another good rule for PowerPoint slides is to **add in pictures or videos** that illustrate your experiment and bring it to life. Be sure to have a brief caption or title on the slide with any pictures or videos that you include along with a reference if needed. It is also acceptable to make a slide with more than one picture on it; just be sure to fit them to a reasonable size on the slide. The nice thing about pictures is that they can capture and create an image or emotion that cannot be easily done with words. Videos are helpful too if they are short, fun to watch, and directly related to your experiment. You can show the experiment room you used or the apparatus that brought your experiment to life. On that note, be careful not to break any confidentiality laws by showing your participants' faces or names in any videos or photographs. Also, make sure to test out your sound before the presentation begins so that you know your video will play properly.

When you are ready to present the results section from your presentation, one of the most important things that you can do with slides is to put your tables and graphs on them using APA or BPS formatting. **Results can be illustrated with a t-table, ANOVA table, or various other types of tables and/or charts. As a researcher who has watched hundreds of presentations, I find that the most important slides are the ones that show that the experiment worked.** It's easy for a researcher to make claims about their research findings, but until they actually show the statistics and let the audience study them, the results won't be truly understood or accepted. Researchers need evidence that they can examine in order to be convinced of its truth; this is just the nature of a researcher's way of thinking. You will want to avoid putting raw data into your slides (or your paper), as it is not meaningful to your audience. What you want to report are your overall statistical results, which we discussed more extensively in Chapter 11.

**As a final note, color is also very important in a presentation.** I would advise using some color and avoid using only grayscale for your slides, as it is drab and boring. Be sure to use colors and contrasts that are easy to read, avoiding too bold or distracting designs. There are few things more frustrating in a presentation than staring at a slide that can't be read or understood. Simplicity is a good approach here.

*Poster Presentations*

There are fewer rules when it comes to creating a poster presentation, but there are also more limitations. There is less that you can do to communicate your research when you use a poster. The basic idea of a poster is that most, if not all, of your research goes onto the poster. You might get up to one minute to talk to a very small audience that passes by your poster, but that's about it. The good news about posters is that they are a lot less stressful to present because they take less time and you usually don't have to stand and speak in front of a large audience.

The home page of Muhlenberg College (2020) provides some good tips for creating a poster presentation. The most important tip is to be sure you have all sections of your research study, such as the abstract, introduction, methods, results, discussion, references, tables and appendices (if relevant), on your poster. Muhlenberg also recommends that you use a large font and a nice color for your pages and/or background poster. Be sure to arrange the sections of your report from top to bottom (see the following illustration), and don't put too much information on your poster.

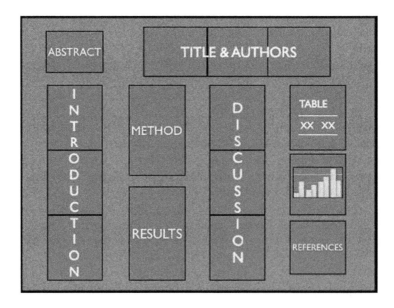

Sample image for a psychology research poster.

Whether you are giving a speech with a PowerPoint presentation or a poster, keep in mind that nobody knows this study like you do. You are the expert, just like a professor. Give your speech with confidence and have fun sharing your knowledge.

## References

Goodreads Inc. (2020). *Jerry Seinfeld Quotes*. www.goodreads.com/ author/quotes/19838. Jerry_Seinfeld

Muhlenberg College. (2020). *Poster Presentation*. www.muhlenberg.edu/ academics/ psychology/posterpresentation/

# 15 Where to Go Next

## Lindsay

Well, now that you have made it through this research methods survival guide, you must be nearing the end of your research methods course. Congratulations! By finishing this class, you have made your future career in psychology possible. Not to mention that you have learned some key concepts that you will likely run into later on, whether in additional college courses or your next job. I will tell you now, most research psychology jobs in today's world will require a master's or doctoral degree. But there are plenty of other job opportunities that you become eligible for after completing your bachelor's degree, including:

*Research Assistant*
*Psychiatric Aide or Attendant*

DOI: 10.4324/9781003099369-15

*Counseling*
*Correctional Treatment Specialist*
*Human Resources Assistant or Advisor*
*Research Analyst*
*Cognitive-Behavioral Health Specialist (I/DD community)*
*Project Evaluator*
*Technical Writer*

These are just some of the jobs you may find available to you, as there are also many other types of jobs (including those outside the realm of psychology) that you may become eligible for once you graduate with a four-year degree:

*Police or Parole Officer*
*Life Coach*
*Criminal Investigator*
*Public Relations Representative*
*Preschool Teacher*
*Special Education Teacher*

As for me, I found myself in a job I never thought I would go into after I graduated with my bachelor's in Psychology. I was all set to attend my same college for their master's program the next fall when I was offered a job as a direct support professional for individuals with intellectual/developmental disabilities in Oregon. Although it was a difficult decision to make, I chose to relocate to Oregon to begin the new job instead of continuing straight into graduate school. I was initially placed in a youth home, but when that wasn't the right fit for me, I was faced with having to be placed elsewhere. Because of my background in psychology, I was able to work in a more selective category of my company, where I now work one-on-one with a young woman with autism. Every day I work with her, I find that I am using knowledge from my years in college, and it helps me better to connect and understand her. Because of this, we have been able to form a strong bond with one another that increases the quality of each of our lives on a daily basis. Although I am still planning on returning to school to pursue research, I am happy to have found a job in which I can use my knowledge of psychology and work closely with such a bright, beautiful mind.

As my personal story conveys, sometimes the job you go into right after graduating college isn't quite the one you expected. But I have found that it is the unexpected happenstances that can end up being the most meaningful. In my case, my current job has taught me more about autism than I ever could have learned in a college classroom, and I am grateful for it every day. Because when the time comes for me to move on and return to school, I will be able to take all of that experience and knowledge with me as I continue into the realm of research.

Those of you who are interested in Clinical Psychology or research will have to embark on a bit of a longer educational journey like I will before becoming qualified to work in such fields. Most students who are interested in either of these two fields will have to make a choice at some point before applying to graduate programs: will I pursue *clinical* psychology or *research* psychology? This is simply because graduate programs differ significantly based on which avenue you choose. After obtaining a BA, psychology students interested in clinical psychology would then have to apply to either a Master's in Marriage and Family Therapy, or a PhD or PsyD in Clinical Psychology. Those that pursue the doctorate are looking at five years of graduate school and then a 3,000-hour internship, followed by a challenging licensing exam. The master's degree involves two years of graduate school, a similar internship, and a licensing exam.

Individuals like myself who choose to go for research instead are looking at a future of 2–5 years in graduate school. But first, you are asked to pick a *specialty*, so to speak. Some of the most common ones include:

*Developmental*
*Cognitive*
*Neuroscience (Biopsychology)*
*Personality*
*Social*
*Industrial/Organizational*
*Sensation & Perception*

Now, beyond choosing a specialty, you will also have to decide what kind of graduate degree you want to get: a *master's* or *doctoral* degree. There are two types of master's degrees you will have to choose from: *Master of Arts (MA)* and *Master of Science (MS)*. The MA degree has a more liberal arts type of focus, which is better for those who plan to go on for a doctorate degree. The MS degree is better for individuals wanting to produce original research, as it is more science focused.

Beyond that, you could even go for a doctoral degree which would qualify you for careers in research, consulting, and teaching. There are currently two types of doctorate degrees you could go for in the field of psychology: *Doctor of Philosophy (PhD)* or *Doctor of Psychology (PsyD)*. Although you will hear many different opinions about the pros and cons of each of these types of programs, what remains constant is what each of them will provide. A PhD program will gear students for a career in conducting research whereas a PsyD program is better for those interested in becoming a therapist.

At this point, there is much for you to consider before choosing your future career path in psychology—granted that it is still your interest. Some students find that following their first research methods course, a career in psychology is not actually what they see themselves doing. That is okay. There are some areas of psychology that are heavy on research and others that are not. Those that pursue an MFT or a PsyD, for example, are typically not looking for careers that are research based.

People that love psychology also go into completely different fields, such as advertising, marketing, and business. The bottom line is that a psychology degree gives you some great skills: people skills as well as statistics and research skills. These can be applicable to many careers, as well as your daily lives. Whatever you decide to do with your career, we both wish you the very best. We know that if you can make it through research methods, you can handle just about any course. Congratulations, you made it!

# Index

For Product Safety Concerns and Information please contact our EU
representative  GPSR@taylorandfrancis.com
Taylor & Francis Verlag GmbH, Kaufingerstraße 24, 80331 München, Germany